STANDING ON MY KNEES

STANDING ON MY KNEES

Establishing a lifeline of prayer

JEFF LUCAS

MONARCH
BOOKS
Oxford, UK & Grand Rapids, Michigan, USA

Previously published by Authentic under the title *How Not to Pray*

Published by Monarch Books
an imprint of
Lion Hudson plc
Wilkinson House, Jordan Hill Road,
Oxford OX2 8DR, England
Email: monarch@lionhudson.com
www.lionhudson.com/monarch

ISBN 978 0 85721 293 1
e-ISBN 978 0 85721 450 8

Acknowledgments
Scripture quotations taken from the Holy Bible, New International Version Anglicised. Copyright © 1979, 1984, 2011 Biblica, formerly International Bible Society. Used by permission of Hodder & Stoughton Ltd, an Hachette UK company. All rights reserved. "NIV" is a registered trademark of Biblica. UK trademark number 1448790.
Scripture quotations marked ESV are from The Holy Bible, English Standard Version® (ESV®) copyright © 2001 by Crossway, a publishing ministry of Good News Publishers. All rights reserved.

Extract page 84 taken from the song "I Will Sing Your Praises" by Ian Smale. Copyright © 1984 Thankyou Music. Adm. by worshiptogether. com songs excl. UK & Europe, admin by Kingswaysongs, a division of David C Cook tym@kingsway.co.uk Used by permission.

A catalogue record for this book is available from the British Library

Printed and bound in the UK, January 2013, LH26.

For Ben, who loves to worship and who is himself
a wonderful answer to prayer.
So glad and grateful that you are part of our
family.

Contents

Introduction 9

1 Lord, teach us how to pray 12

2 We *can* pray 22

3 Prayer is not a lengthy speech 35

4 The power of shared prayer 48

5 The alphabet of prayer begins with F for Father 67

6 God is right here, right now 88

7 Prayer: it's not just about us 101

8 Prayer: it is about us 121

9 We, the forgiven, pass forgiveness around 136

10 Come to God, whatever the season 158

Introduction: Standing on my knees

When Sarah Kelly sings, people listen with their hearts as well as their ears.

There's something not just about her voice but about the singer herself that reaches out and grabs you: listen up, now. The voice *is* arresting, at times a gentle whisper, and then suddenly a rich, throaty roar, a textured sound so distinctive, it's little wonder that the makers of *Grey's Anatomy* often use Sarah's songwriting and voice to create a dramatic musical backdrop.

But Sarah Kelly is more than a voice. Look past her bubbly, wide-eyed, almost little-girl-lost persona. This little girl is anything but lost. A leading figure in the American Christian music scene, she's not just earning a crust turning out winsome spiritual ditties that rhyme but don't actually mean much. Sarah took what is supposed to be the yellow brick road to happiness: Christian girl marries Christian boy, and hand in hand, they both live happily ever after. But that hopeful road turned out to be a highway to domestic hell, and she became a victim of physical abuse. Today, she could be jaded and disillusioned, faith pummelled out of her by repeated spite. But instead, she is still vibrant, trusting, hopeful again. She decided to trust God when everything went bad. And that's why I sat up and listened hard when I heard her song, "Standing on my knees". Nothing trite about it, as if prayer produces instant sunshine into every day, this is a song about discovering strength and grace when the weather turns very ugly. Consider the words:

I've been swept away by a hurricane
But I landed on my feet.
It happened fast and all I know
Is I'm where I need to be, yeah,
I'm where I need to be, yeah.

Empty handed and free,
I'm still standing, still standing.
'Cause you are strong when I'm weak,
so I'm still standing, still standing on my knees.

It's hard to guess where the road will lead next
But I'm up for every turn.
I know you're near to make my way clear,
As I live and as I learn,
As I live and as I learn.

Empty handed and free,
I'm still standing, still standing.
'Cause you are strong when I'm weak,
so I'm still standing, still standing.

And life left me jaded and numb from this fight,
But you've brought a second chance
At a first try tonight.

Empty handed and free,
I'm still standing, still standing.
'Cause you are strong when I'm weak,
so I'm still standing, still standing.

Empty handed and free,
I'm still standing, I'm still standing,
'Cause you are strong when I'm weak,
so I'm still standing, still standing on my knees.

Sarah's song, and the journey that forged the song in a furnace of pain, is a perfect context for this book. The premise is simple, and yet it's one that I most easily tend to forget. You and I are not called to tough it out and stand on our own two feet, but to discover grace and strength in the place of prayer – standing on our knees. As we'll see, that's not to suggest that kneeling is the only posture required for praying, but the metaphor is helpful. I'm grateful that Sarah has made the song available for download without charge to the readers of this book. Why not pause, go online, and listen to that voice and that heart. (This can be found at www.sarahkelly.com/standing with the password "prayer" – do take some time to browse her site and other music too.)

And as we share these reflections about prayer together, may they help you, In some way, to discover what it means to stand on your knees too.

Jeff Lucas
Bury, Sussex, 2012

1

Lord, teach us how to pray...

Well done, you.

Hearty congratulations, because you, sturdy soul that you are, have plucked a book off the shelf that includes the word "prayer" in its subtitle. This was brave of you: I normally run from books about prayer myself. I'm usually overwhelmed by the heady mixture of inspiration and intimidation that mugs me in turn whenever I read about prayer.

The books on prayer that both thrill and terrify me are often well written, carefully researched, meticulously punctuated, and peppered with multitudinous Bible references. They include accounts of epic answers to prayer that should nudge me into praying more than I do, and are stacked with breathless sentences that end with exclamation marks (as in *breathless sentences that end with exclamation marks!!*). I don't usually doubt the authenticity of the sensational stories that are recounted, although those who insist that they regularly bump into angels before breakfast do make me wonder.

But my main problem is that books about prayer are usually written by people who are quite good at praying. It makes perfect sense, but is so unhelpful. Want a book about swimming? Hire Michael Phelps, not me. I've never even mastered the front crawl – it's a challenge of coordination. It's useful if the author of a cookery book can actually fry an egg, or even crack it open without breaking the yolk. Usually, I can't. Books should be written by those who have a good grasp of their subject. But when it comes to prayer, some "experts" don't equip me, but edge me into paralysis instead. I get a few pages in, thrill to a few *dramatic stories!!,* and then feel like a twenty-five-stone arthritic in a Manchester United shirt, playing against David Beckham at Wembley. It's not a good feeling.

The intimidation reaches dangerous levels when the book talks about any kind of *extended* prayer. By extended, I mean anything over fifteen minutes or so. Even as I use the phrase *extended time of prayer,* I blush with shame. Years ago, as an excited pastor desperately in search of some exclamation marks, I joined three other ministers in a misguided effort to provoke God into doing something scintillating. We solemnly informed our bemused spouses that we were going to lock ourselves away in a room, where we would continuously pray and fast for days, even weeks, if necessary, until we saw some kind of spiritual breakthrough. I'm not exactly sure how we were going to know that the much-desired breakthrough had been achieved, but our lack of thoughtful preparation was eclipsed by our enthusiasm. Like most eclipses, it didn't last long. The "marathon" actually endured for about three hours, by which time I was ready for a cheese and tomato sandwich and a comfortable bed. I blush deeper red as I remember that it was I who announced in a sonorous, "I've had a revelation" voice that I "sensed" that our prayer time had achieved what was needed, which was probably driven by my previously mentioned need for Cheddar. I smile when I recall how utterly relieved the other three erstwhile intercessors were, absolutely delighted to disperse and head home, job done. Our spouses welcomed us with feigned surprise.

Others who have done so much better with lengthy seasons of prayer don't always help me. In researching for this book, I pored over the biographical details of one jolly chap who followed Jesus a hundred years before anything was on television, who passed his days in thrilled solitude, and who was in the habit of crawling into a hollow log for weeks of uninterrupted intercession. This story of log burrowing was supposed to cheer me up and encourage me to head for the woods myself, but instead, I felt profoundly discouraged. I know I wouldn't last thirty minutes in the bowels of an intercessory tree, and the only "deep ministry" that would result would be the woodlice investigating my underwear. Start talking casually about "the devotional life", and I get that weary feeling that I experienced when my school report included the comment scrawled in angry red ink: *"C+. Could do better."*

Just the other day, I discovered William Penn's

description of the Quaker leader George Fox. It was both awe-inspiring and daunting.

> Above all, he excelled in prayer. The inwardness and
> weight of his spirit, the reverence and solemnity
> of his dress and behaviour, and the fewness and
> fullness of his words, have often struck even
> strangers with admiration... The most awful, living,
> reverent frame I ever felt or beheld, I must say, was
> in his prayer.[1]

There is no doubting the huge heart of Fox. His life provides rich inspiration for those who want to go beyond superficiality and trite spirituality and find a deeper walk with God. But then I read the description of him again, and am intimidated by Fox's consistent self-discipline. I ponder his "fewness and fullness" of words and immediately know that all too often chatter gushes out of my mouth with the speed and control of Niagara Falls. And his weighty spirit? Mine is sometimes so lean, I think it's been to *Weight Watchers.*

I write daily Bible reading notes, but wonder if I would read the Bible daily if I didn't write the notes. Every year on New Year's Eve I enter into solemn vows that include planning to read my Bible right through, and then I invariably come unstuck in the gall bladders of Leviticus or the family trees of Chronicles and Kings. I'm currently developing a *Read through the Bible in 300 years* course...

Writers of books about prayer often live in an

---

1   Samuel Janney, *The Life of George Fox*, originally published 1858, republished 2003, Kessinger Publishing, p. 30.

emotional, spiritual land called *Utter Certainty*. This bold, superlative location is a doubtless zone; awkward questions about pain, suffering, and why my car broke down last month (just after I'd abandoned my roadside assistance insurance) have no place there. I do have occasional day trips to *Utter Certainty*, and it's a luxurious resort: I'd like to move in and set up home permanently. Fog is banished in that endlessly summery place, and every detail of the landscape is drawn in bold, solid lines. I would like to make *Utter Certainty* my home.

But then there are some days – more than I'd like to admit – when I find myself meandering off, like a sheep, to camp out for a while on the chilly, bleak moors of an inhospitable location called *Where on earth am I and, by the way, where has God gone?* It's as far away from *Utter Certainty* as Hawaii is from the Antarctic. In *Certainty*, the paths are solid underfoot, and well signposted, but in *Where on earth,* crumbling, unmarked paths snake across impossibly high cliff edges, where just one slip would mean a fatal fall. There are treacherous quicksands that threaten to suck me under for ever, and familiar landmarks disappear in the swirling mists. It's a place that's about as warm and friendly as the set of *The Hound of the Baskervilles*. I stumble on, hoping to spot a welcome light to lead me home. The bitter cold snaps at my fingers and toes, and I long for a guide – or God – to get me out of that wasteland.

Ironically, as I begin this book, I am currently on one such camping trip. I am in two locations at once: in *Where on earth am I and, by the way, where has God gone?* and also parked in the innards of a large British Airways jet which is aimed at America. I shall shortly be dispensing large chunks of biblical teaching to some assorted gatherings of nice Christian people. The fact that they have invited me to fly over for a chat creates massive pressure. Theirs is a special event, which means that I need to say something special. Even as I tap away, I am being whisked through the sky at 500 miles per hour, my trajectory carefully navigated by computers, enabling Nigel the pilot to announce the time of our projected touchdown to within a minute or two, even though we are still 3,000 miles from our destination.

But the laws of physics and the precision genius of computer chips do not govern my emotional and spiritual condition. Right now, while wrestling with a bland Chicken Caesar salad at 36,000 feet, I feel less certain about my own ability to do anything useful for Jesus. I'm not sure who I doubt more – him or me.

I look around the cabin, survey the backs of the heads of my fellow passengers, and suddenly feel unsettled about my faith. What do they do to cause this spiritual nervous tic? Simple. They unnerve me because of their *normality*. They sit and nurse their plastic cups and appear to have no concerns about holiness or morality, about the meaning and purpose of life or the life-exploding eruption that breaks upon a person when they discover that there is a Creator alive and well at the heart of the universe. I see no signs of fretfulness on their faces because of the niggling impotence of the church that professes Christ's name so boldly but sometimes witnesses to his life so pathetically. No, they just sit there, investigating their peanuts, living another hour without apparent depth or significance, mesmerized by just existing. For a moment, I envy them, and feel that to believe all of the time is too much like hard work. I wriggle here in my torturous airline seat, silently wrestling with a few of the deeper questions of life. Why do the good suffer? How can prayer interact with a sovereign God, and what does sovereignty mean anyway? What happens to Muslims when they die? And why are all pilots called Nigel?

My fellow passengers seem immune to the assaults of these bruising questions. Round and round, the confused, fearful thoughts tumble in my brain, while some of the other passengers shake their plastic cups with annoyance because their ice is melting. And I shake my head in vain, hoping to dispel some of the ether inside my skull, but it persists, and God seems a long way off. A few moments of reflection will cause me to realize that actually, to live life for nothing, to merely survive, is no blessing. And who am I to judge that the ice-jigglers are superficial souls without purpose or conviction? But in the tired, mildly depressed condition that long plane flights create in me, I feel battered by the turbulence of uncertainty and disorientation.

The plane zooms effortlessly forward, a precision dart on course for its destination. I wish that my progress and ultimate arrival could be predicted with similar accuracy.

All this is said, dear reader, to let you know that I write this book not as an expert on life, on all things spiritual, but as a bumpkin doing his best – sometimes – to be a follower and an apprentice of Jesus. Get the message? Put your intimidation away: this book is not written by an expert on the subject of prayer.

Perhaps you're still not convinced, so I'll say just a little more.

I fall asleep when I pray. I read about the three closest friends of Jesus, continually nodding off in Gethsemane, and am glad that it's included in the story. I'm in good company.

I'm inconsistent when it comes to worship. Occasionally I find myself overwhelmed with praise for God, which flows out of me in spontaneous thanksgiving, a gushing well. Sometimes that worship is diminished to the *plop, plop, plop* of a dripping tap, the last dregs of rust-stained water, clogged in the pipes. Being of charismatic persuasion, I sometimes speak in tongues when I pray, believing this to be a language of the Holy Spirit. This too is erratic, at times allowing me to sing out a serenade to God without intelligible words, a passionate, intimate offering. At other times, this practice leaves me feeling that I am chanting some bizarre mantra that has got about as much passion as the recitation of a railway timetable.

OK, enough already. Perhaps I've overdone things, and you're now wondering what on earth I could say that could help you to pray. Why should you buy this book? Well, first of all, let me say without hesitation that it is God's perfect will that you make this purchase (only kidding). Seriously, I'd like to invite you to join me, and join the crowd who wander up to Jesus and say, perhaps pathetically, "Lord, teach us how to pray." I'd like to ask you to grab a coffee, pull up a chair, and take a good look at this business of praying, because I remain convinced that Jesus wants us to pray. He assumed three things of his followers in the Sermon on the Mount: that we would pray, fast, and walk alongside the poor in generous service. He is still accepting applications from would-be learners like you and me, and wants to help us to move forward in our praying.

Some of us don't pray much, and it's not because dark and diabolical forces are camped out in our bathrooms, conspiring to stamp out our praying. Rather, the enemy of prayer is contained between our ears. Strongholds, castles of thoughts, have been steadily built in our minds over the years, subtle and obvious deceptions that militate against our praying and defeat us before we start. The shorthand word that I'd like to use for these strongholds is *myths*. Perhaps some of them truly are engineered in hell, but for the most part, we have built our own sandcastles. That's why some churches don't require any spiritual attack whatsoever in order to be rendered ineffective. All the seeds of their impotency are deeply planted in the individual and collective consciousness of their members. They are brought down, defeated by their own thinking.

So, as we think about standing on our knees, I'd like to examine a few of those myths and see if we can clear the building sites of our minds, and in doing so perhaps find ourselves praying better – even later today, or tomorrow perhaps. The basis for our journey is the Lord's Prayer – or the disciples' prayer – or the Lord's model prayer. Hey, I don't really care what you call it, it's the familiar one that begins "Our Father" – and you'll remember that it goes like this (don't skip over this bit please... caught you...):

> *Our Father in heaven,*
> *hallowed be your name,*
> *your kingdom come,*
> *your will be done,*
> *on earth as it is in heaven.*
> *Give us today our daily bread.*
> *Forgive us our debts,*
> *as we also have forgiven our debtors.*
> *And lead us not into temptation,*
> *but deliver us from the evil one. (Matthew 6:9-13)*

OK, let's go. Onward, through the fog.

2

We *can* pray

"When you pray…"

Ever find yourself looking around on Sunday morning, during worship, and checking out fellow members of your congregation? I am an avid student of people (that's a nice way of saying I'm nosey) and so do this more than I should, with a variety of results. Sometimes I feel a warm sense of gratitude as I peruse the family of Christians that God has given me – what a fine, fun lot they are! Well, most of them…

But I'm guessing that much of the time, when we survey the home crowd that is our local church, we feel that everyone is superior to us. Most Christians, sadly, are quite good at feeling bad. Surely, we reason, everyone else has read Ecclesiastes through twice this morning and has Solomon's musings all figured out. They must have a wi-fi efficient prayer line, constantly connected at an impossibly high speed. We reason that their hearts are less likely to be sullied by fear, doubt, lust, anxiety, and angst at the size of Betty's hat (the straw fruit bowl that is blocking our view). We alone are the solitary lowlife types who wrestle with such carnality. This same tendency towards self-dismissal and the feeling that "I alone can't do it" kicks in when it comes to thinking about prayer.

We can nurse the idea that *everyone else* is adept at praying, but we have the franchise on failure when it comes to personal spirituality. Crises break out deep inside the heads and hearts of people who attend those long prayer meetings that are so mind-numbingly boring, they carry a whiff of penance: we feel good because we've endured something so bad. After what seems the twentieth hour (even though we've only actually been there for twenty minutes) we risk opening our eyes to take a quick glance at our watches during a snore-inducing prayer that is nudging angels to take a nap. It is then that we imagine, with a major pang of inferiority, that everyone else in the place is hurtling along the intercessory information superhighway with apparent ease. There is no trouble with a meandering mind for them, no momentary lapses of concentration threatening their unbroken harmony with heaven, no drifting into wondering what's going to happen next in *EastEnders*.

The truth is, we all struggle, and that knowledge alone can be liberating. There are no live inhabitants of planet Earth who currently do not have "flesh" – and the Bible makes it clear that whatever our great aspirations, the spirit is willing and the flesh is weak. Struggles in prayer are not symptoms of some creeping spiritual disease in our lives, or authentic evidence to confirm our fears that we really are third-class disciples. Rather, the challenge to pray that we all face is simply evidence of two facts:

1. We are alive (hence the flesh is operating).
2. Jesus hasn't come back yet (hence we are still struggling).

Spiritually speaking, we are currently on the dark side of the moon, and radio communication is, at best, patchy. That doesn't mean that God is distant, as we'll see later. But daily we contend with the "interference" that comes from having to live by faith. One day, we will see Jesus with the 20/20 clarity of eternity, and in that dawning vision everything else will become clear; obscurity and mystery will snap into focus. In the meantime, we peer through grubby double glazing (my paraphrase of "Now we see through a glass, darkly"). Not to be able to see it all as we would like should come as no surprise to us. God knows our struggles, and the Bible is candid about our ineptitude. "We do not know what we ought to pray for" (Romans 8:26) has become one of my favourite verses of Scripture. Far from condemning us for our half-sight, God recognizes the limitations of our current condition. This is the reality for us all: not just for you.

The ecstasy and the agony

"But what about Norman the bionic pray-er?" I hear you protest. Perhaps there is a supersonic prayer warrior in your church, who seems able to soar into spiritual ionospheres while you chug along in a desperate attempt to get your ancient prayer biplane off the ground. It coughs and splutters and barely lifts its old tyres three feet off the runway. Then it crashes back down again in bone-jarring defeat, while Norman zips by you with jet-propelled ease...

Yes, there are some people who are *very* good at prayer – and some who have a particular calling to pray. They often write those books about prayer that I mentioned earlier. I read the stories of epic prayer heroes such as Rees Howells or John "Praying" Hyde (good job his last name wasn't "Mantis") and feel like a prayer novice trembling before an intercessory master. But may I put it bluntly? *Those stories aren't completely true.* Some biographical writing about prayer is blessedly peppered with sweat, tears, and disappointment, wonderfully balancing the epic with the mundane. But often we only get the edited victory reports, and they aren't the whole story.

Something similar happens in public meetings when someone shares a blessing that God has given them or some answer to prayer. Am I suggesting that these stories are all embellished or exaggerated? In most cases, the stories are genuine. With the exception of those rabid evangelistic types who led six million people to Jesus in the supermarket last Saturday – before they'd even got their shopping – most people tell the truth when they talk about their friendship with God. But the sharing often only spotlights the *successes* in prayer. Simple limitations of time mean that we don't get to hear about the other prayers that seemed to be met with a stony lack of response. We hear about the ecstasy, but little of the agony.

The problem is further compounded in that, in some churches, to say your prayers are not apparently being answered would be considered to be a "negative confession", a betrayal that would let the side down. This is madness.

Sometimes Norman the bionic prayer warrior will resort to clichés, which are good for squeezing out a few murmured "Amens" from the congregation but leave me baffled. An obvious example can be found in reports of answered prayer. "Everybody in my office went down with a nasty dose of bubonic plague last week," cries Norman with gusto. "The streets were absolutely clogged with hearse carts and the sounds of people screaming, 'Bring out your dead!' I, Norman, however, did not go down with any nasty boils or plague-like symptoms. The Lord has spared me from this wicked curse. *Isn't the Lord good?*"

Yes, I want to shout, the Lord is good – and I'm delighted, Norman, to hear of your deliverance in the boil department. But is the Lord only *good* when we're spared? Christians died in the unspeakably ugly tragedy that unravelled on our television screens when New York's Twin Towers were devastated by terrorist-steered planes. Was the Lord having an off day – or being *bad* perhaps? I don't believe so. Across this world today, countless Christians are separated from their families because of their faith, battling with fear while waiting for test results, or staring at lengthy courses of treatment and an uncertain medical future. Let's be careful with a slogan theology that seems to imply God is only on form when the sun is shining. Not only will we get disappointed, but also others who are trying to find their way home through a rainstorm can get very hurt indeed.

I was so refreshed to read of the journey of Sharon and Hugo Anson, who were childless for twelve years. Their primary battle was with cliché-wielding Christians – but their faith shines with hope mingled with reality.

> People would occasionally prophesy over us,
> telling us we would have a child. It felt like all
> the pain people had experienced through once
> being childless came out on us. I found that very
> abusive. People would say the reason we were not
> having children was because of pride or because
> we were more interested in our ministry than in
> having a family. Part of me wanted to tell them
> the medical facts, but another part didn't bother
> trying to explain…[2]

I'm so thankful for the brutal honesty of the New Testament. Paul the apostle is never presented as a swashbuckling superhero, despite his huge achievements. He writes to the contentious Corinthians and lets them know of his weariness and depression – feeling as one who is under "the sentence of death" (2 Corinthians 1:9). Jesus didn't skip towards Golgotha. He kneels beneath gargantuan, back-breaking agony, overwhelmed by the sorrow and pain that is about to break over him and may crush him.

Jesus is the victor – and victory requires battle. Battle is not a precise, antiseptic science, but the ebb and flow of breakthrough and wounding, of the adrenalin rush that

---

2   *Christianity and Renewal*, January 2002.

comes from winning and the bone-numbing weariness that comes from slogging it out for another hour. All of this was true of Jesus: and it's true of Norman too, whether he admits it or not.

The past doesn't determine the future

Remember that intoxicating enthusiasm that you felt when you became a Christian? For me, it was the most breathtaking, exhilarating time of my life. I was so desperate to let people know that I had found God that I'm sure I was probably totally off-putting to most. I had a gigantic Jesus badge on my lapel, and there were so many plastic fishes plastered across the back of my car, it resembled a mobile aquarium. Subtlety was not a consideration.

My early attempts at sharing my faith consisted of a breathless monologue, in which I would misquote a lengthy string of Scriptures. But while I was short on biblical accuracy, I was loaded with enthusiasm. Why the wondrous thrill? Part of it was the joy of discovery. The Bible was a sparkling treasure chest brimming over with priceless gems of truth. I couldn't understand most of it, and couldn't tell the difference between the Old Testament, the New Testament, and the maps at the back, but the thrill of being on this brand new spiritual safari was intoxicating. But another source of the bubbling joy was the sheer luxury of being able to look at the future with hope: what I had been in the past was not going to dictate my future any more. Why, I was a brand new creation in Christ – now, everything was possible. I was filled with hope. A delightful springtime season of change was in the air.

A distant cousin of this hope for change can be found every New Year's Eve. Thousands throng the streets for the big countdown to midnight, and while for some it is little more than another reason to escape into an alcohol-induced haze, for many the birth of a new year signals the possibility that life might yet be different. The chimes at midnight signal, we hope and pray, the advent of a yet unstained year, for at least a second or two. Perhaps the world will be more peaceful; perhaps we, with our resolutions, might be a little more loving, healthy, rich, content, thin, or successful. For many brand new Christians, hope for change is a major source of joy. Why, they are going to be altered – and they believe that they will alter their world as a result.

But then new Christians settle down. Sometimes they land with a huge bump, shot out of the sky by the lack of hope and joy exhibited by Christians who have been around for a while. The Bible becomes something you read because that's what Christians do, isn't it? The voyage of discovery descends into a tedious maintenance programme. And one of the most tragic casualties of this settling is hope. We give up believing that we can change the world – or indeed that we can be changed. Stuck in a groove, we peer at the future through the sad eyes of those who are condemned to be for ever the same. A leopard can't change its spots, we insist. As we settle into that shadowy land, we are prey to all kinds of temptations. Hope, however, is the moral force that acts as a crash barrier, bouncing me back from the cliff side when I would rather throw myself headfirst into the temporary insanity of sin. Hope is the engine that keeps us walking forward to another day, believing that we can yet be transformed, albeit slowly and painfully, into a better, stronger person than we are now.

But a hiss from hell tells me that I will never be better or stronger than I am, that holiness is a doctrine that I fear but could never be a reality that I can actually experience. I am crushed into believing that I might just as well get on with being who I am, and sin away. My failure and judgment are inevitable anyway, so what's the point of any attempt towards moral heroism? I am doomed to be as I am – or so I am deluded into thinking.

Peter, the once-hopeful fisherman, was mugged by hopelessness. Even after three breathtaking years in the company of Jesus, Peter sulked and descended into a deep, shame-shrouded despair. His problems were not generated by a suicidal angst with the world, but by a gaze into his inner world. But a brief breakfast with Jesus changed all of that. Peter was not destined to go down in history as a failure forever with the word "denial" tattooed on his forehead, but as the fearless apostle in whose shadow power and healing throbbed. A thousand resurrections are possible. What has been does not have to be in the future: you and I can change. We are followers of the One who transforms.

Prayer is learned

Some actions in life come naturally to healthy human beings – bowel movements, breathing, and blinking, for example, are some of the fundamental mechanisms of physical existence. But most of the basic actions of bodily coordination are the result of learning and practice. Moving the limbs is an unlearned reflex, but coordinating that movement into the effortless grace of walking requires a lot of training and practice – and not a few heavy crash landings on one's backside in the process.

We can labour under the impression that prayer is simply doing what comes naturally. After all, we love Jesus, don't we – so therefore prayer *ought* to be easier than it is. Really? Just how natural is it to have what is occasionally (let's get real – most of the time) a one-sided conversation with someone that you can't see? The truth is that *all* communication is the result of a journey of learning, be it in the development of vocabulary and expression, the understanding of body language and how it relates to our communication, or the more subtle arts of tact, diplomacy, and timing.

Prayer is not as easy as breathing: it is the fruit of committed apprenticeship. Thus the disciples asked Jesus to teach them how to pray. Paul encourages Timothy to "train" himself in godliness (1 Timothy 4:8) – the Greek word used there is *gumnasia*, from which we get our word "gymnasium".

As a card-carrying member of the local gym who for years demonstrated my commitment to regular attendance by the payment of high annual fees – and actually showing up there twice in two years – I can testify to the fact that, most of the time, I don't really feel like donning my sports kit and heading to the torture chamber. Gyms aren't made for people who always feel like working out (although I understand that exercise can be addictive – a life-controlling force that I've never personally struggled with). Rather, the gym requires perseverance, energy, and a refusal to give up even though you're surrounded by muscle-bound gods who apparently bench-press large trucks. Running a marathon isn't easy. Lifting heavy weights takes practice. And prayer is a skill we need to grow in, not one that we're born with.

Something old, something new, something borrowed...

We can think that we're bad at praying, whereas actually it's our methods and approaches to prayer that have become tedious and worn out. We're not bad, just bored. I'm going to say it now, and don't throw those stones at me, please: the practice of prayer can be boring. It isn't easy settling yourself down for a warm conversation with an invisible Friend. It's wonderful when we can approach these encounters with faith and expectancy, but there are times when it seems a ridiculous exercise, talking to One who doesn't appear to respond – at least not in the immediate conversational sense. Prayer is sometimes exhilarating, and sometimes a bit like having a good chat with the ceiling. Are our words even penetrating the plaster?

I've discovered, however, that we can grow in prayer as we use different approaches to it. For some time, since a friendly bishop introduced me to it, I've been using the Anglican prayer book as a basis for my prayers, sometimes first thing in the morning and sometimes in the closing moments before sleep. It's taken me a while to get used to opening a prayer book. First of all, I had problems knowing where I was in the seasons of the so-called Christian year. I knew about Advent (all those cardboard calendars with little doors you open and chocolate treats to scoff), but beyond that I am all at sea when it comes to Epiphanies and high days and holidays. The idea of what seemed like sanctified script-reading from an "Ancient and Modern" autocue didn't appeal to a spontaneity-obsessed nonconformist like me. But I pressed through, and, in encountering the power of liturgy, I made the simple discovery that I don't pray more than I do *because I simply can't think of anything useful to say.* It has added another dimension to my spirituality, to take the carefully shaped words of another, the fruits of meditation and reflection that leap and dance with biblical truth, that have been the comfort of believers through the centuries. I've discovered the thrill of approaching my spirituality in a different way. To insist that we always pray the same way is as boring as eating the same meal over and over, or insisting that lovemaking must always follow precisely the same pattern. This is a predictability that makes the divine dull. It's a tragedy, as Annie Dillard laments:

Week after week I was moved by the pitiableness of
the bare linoleum floored sacristy which no flowers
could cheer or soften, by the terrible singing
I so loved, by the fatigued Bible readings, the
lagging emptiness and dilution of the liturgy, the
horrifying vacuity of the sermon, and by the fog of
senselessness pervading the whole, which existed
alongside, and probably caused, the wonder of the
fact that we came; we returned; we showed up;
week after week we went through with it.[3]

Is our prayer life in the doldrums? Why don't we sit down for
a few minutes and ask whether it's not that *prayer* is boring
– perhaps *we* are. Do you always kneel to pray? Then go
for a walk. Is your praying of the loud, aggressive *"God isn't
deaf but he isn't nervous either, so there"* kind? Then give your
mouth a well-earned vacation and try the sound of silence.
Do you consider icons and images to be the stamping ground
of sincerely misled idolaters? Well, lighten up, literally. Break
out a candle and let its flickering flame warm your soul. Do
something different, for God's sake. Literally. And for your
sake too.

You can pray. And you can grow in prayer.

---

3   Annie Dillard, *Teaching a Stone to Talk*, New York: HarperCollins, 1982.

3

Prayer is not a lengthy speech

"When you pray, say…"

"Pray as you can, and not as you can't."

– Dom Chapman

The heaters were ancient, ugly contraptions that hung down from the ceilings of the tin-roofed mission church. Switched on and off by a lingering chain, they hissed and crackled during our services, and produced comfort and torture in turn. Their smell was the welcome scent of the familiar, like dusty books in libraries or roast potatoes on Sundays. It spoke to us, announcing the glad news that we were together again for our weekly celebration, when we stepped out of our confusing worlds and gathered to peer at a heavenly vision.

Pensioners forgot their bills and aches and pains, and youngsters laid aside their fear of spots and being uncool. We tiptoed into the presence of God with our loud songs and our hopeful hands raised skyward.

*Let the fire fall, let the fire fall, let the fire from
   heaven fall!*
*We are waiting, and expecting, now in faith, dear Lord,
   we call.*
*Let the fire fall, let the fire fall, on Thy promise we
   depend;*
*With the Holy Ghost from heaven let the Pentecostal
   fire descend.*

Those services were filled with beautiful moments, when it
seemed that God was walking around the place, hugs and
smiles scattered everywhere as he did so.

Nearly four decades later, I can still hear the poetry
of their prayers as if it were yesterday. Many of them were
rough and ready East Enders who felt that God should be
addressed in a posher voice than their own. Like my own,
their natural speech was a little short on "h" sounds. "'Ow
are yer, mate? 'Orrible weather, don't yer fink?" is perhaps a
slight exaggeration, but Henry Higgins would have had a
nightmare with our church, for whom the rain in Spain did
not fall gently on the plain, if you get my drift. I remember
them with huge fondness and great appreciation: what
wonderful friends of God – and to me – they were.

But our prayers must have sounded like the mock-
pompous voice of a haughty butler: "Great and gracious
hah-heavenly Father, we come into Thy presence today
in the most mighty and, hem, majestic name of Jesus…"
Some of us pronounced the Lord's name as *Yay-zuss,* which
implied that we were fluent in Hebrew or at least had been

to Israel for our holidays...

We weren't being pretentious, just respectful. Of course, God wanted to hear us just as we were: no elocution lessons were required. But I remember the lilting rise and fall of our East End voices as people poured out their hearts to God at great length. We would quote reams of Scripture with fluent ease. Some would quietly weep; this was no empty emotionalism, but the fruit of genuine love for the Lord Jesus. Many of these folks had been dealt a difficult hand in life, but theirs was a simple trust in God. Their love for Jesus drew me like a moth to light, but I just couldn't ever aspire to their praying technique. And they never demanded that I did. I would sometimes get to my feet during the prayer meeting and pray loudly the most absurd and ridiculous tosh. Next to our church building there stood a bus stop, which gave me a lovely opportunity to pray, with great gusto, "Save all those people on the bus, Lord. Fill 'em with the Holy Ghost! Heal any sick people on the bus! Raise the dead on the bus!" Those prayer "warriors", as we used to call them, refused to allow me to be intimidated by my lack of thoughtfulness; they inspired but never crushed new Christians.

I can't pray like that...

I think that the disciples of Jesus probably felt intimidated by others who were apparently better at prayer than they were. Perhaps they shifted uncomfortably in their half-sleep on those days when Jesus stirred himself in the crisp cold of the dawning hours and wandered off to confer with his Father about the coming day. Did they feel some pang of guilt as they turned over and huddled back down to catch some more sleep? None of the disciples came from a background of practised spirituality – they were amateurs at prayer, and asked their master to teach them how to do it (Luke 11:1).

I imagine that they would have been intimidated by the eloquence and dress-to-impress piety of the Pharisees who prayed at volume on the street corners. These trained experts in public prayer were required to pray for a minimum of three hours each day. Their silver-tongued petitions would have made the friends of Jesus shrink as they struggled to make sense of prayer.

The rabbis were convinced that the only good praying was long praying – Jesus links their wide-open mouths with their inflated egos: "The teachers of the law... for a show make lengthy prayers" (Mark 12:38–40). In some churches, a similar idea still exists, even if only at a subconscious level. If you're going to pray privately, it had better be for at least an hour, and preferably at an unearthly time in the morning. While it *is* good to set quality time aside to spend with God, the bitter irony is that often, because we feel that we can't pray for an hour, we don't pray at all. Isn't it better to *pray* for five minutes than to *aspire to pray* for an hour (and indeed passionately believe that hour-long praying is the way to go) but not pray at all? If we have this "never mind the quality, feel the width" approach to prayer, then we miss out on the opportunity of just being with Jesus for brief but vital prayerful conversations.

Prayer as technique

In some senses, prayer is a technique, an art, a skill, in the same way that all communication is a learned skill — we established that in the last chapter. But we can become obsessed with the mechanism of communication rather than the person with whom we are communicating. Richard Foster points out that we are in a danger zone whenever we become preoccupied with spiritual discipline in and of itself rather than preoccupied with the God whom we meet through the disciplines.

> It is a pitfall to view the disciplines as virtuous in themselves. In and of themselves, the disciplines have no virtue, possess no righteousness, contain no rectitude. It was this important truth that the Pharisees failed to see. The disciplines place us before God; they do not give us Brownie points with God.[4]

Women sometimes complain that men are often more preoccupied with sexual technique than lovemaking. These men view the distant orgasm as the ultimate tape to be breasted at the conclusion of an epic performance. In a spirit of competitiveness, and macho pride, they insist that only a medal-winning display is good enough, whereas their partner wants real closeness, warmth — and not necessarily an award-winning encounter. Sex like this is reduced to athletically

---

4   Richard Foster, *Prayer: Finding the Heart's True Home*, London: Hodder and Stoughton, 1992.

ᴘling rather than real lovemaking – and ᴛh whom we engage in sex is not so much a more an apparatus, available for the slaking of a ᴍe-fed thirst. In some cases, once the performance is oᴠ, tragically, the human "apparatus" can be discarded. An unhealthy preoccupation with technique can develop even in the strongest marriages.

In just the same way, there's a danger that we can almost worship prayer itself, as if the pursuit of prayer as a habit carries its own rewards. We are thus engaging in spirituality, but a self-directed spirituality. It does not cause us to bump into God, but allows us to feel we have done our duty. The task has been completed, the checklist ticked – but we have still not engaged with God by faith. Similar things happen in worship: the practice of "worshipping worship" is common today.

But… prayer *is* a discipline

While *technique* should not be our priority, we will nevertheless need to embrace discipline if we are to pray at all. But "discipline" is not a popular word these days. It conjures up images of wide-eyed, staring fanatics from the past – and there have been a few. They can't be faulted for their commitment, but may have been a bit short-changed when wisdom was being handed out.

The fourth-century monk Macarius of Alexandria ate no cooked food for seven years. Deliberately exposing his naked body to poisonous flies, he slept in a marsh for six months. Some ascetics could boast that they had not lain down to sleep for fifty years. Others kept a record of how many years it had been since they had even set eyes upon a woman.

Simeon Stylites (AD 390–459) famously built a column six feet high in the Syrian desert. He became dissatisfied with its size and found one sixty feet high, and three feet across, where he sat in splendid isolation. On this perch Simeon lived for thirty years, exposed to rain and sun and cold. A ladder enabled disciples to take him food and remove his waste. He bound himself to the pillar by a rope, which became embedded in his flesh and putrefied around it. The result stank, and teemed with worms, perhaps causing those bemused spectators at the foot of the pillar to rejoice that the reeking Simeon had chosen to live aloft. It is said that Simeon picked up the worms which fell from his sores and replaced them there, saying to them, "Eat what God has given you." Yuk.

The Irish saint Finnchua was a lot of fun too. He spent seven years suspended by his armpits in iron shackles. He and St Ite deliberately allowed their bodies to be eaten by beetles.

And then there was St Ciaran, who mixed his bread with sand, and St Kevin (I'm not making this up, honest), who refused to sit down for seven years. Wearing hair shirts, self-flagellation, and involuntary dancing were all practices embraced by the rival orders of St Francis and St Dominic. The lovely but grubby Clarissa never washed any part of her body after her conversion except her fingertips. Probably not a popular house guest, she reportedly "dropped vermin while she walked".

These follies and excesses led many of the reformers to reject the idea of disciplined spirituality – particularly those who had come from such an ascetic background. Martin Luther despised the concept of spiritual disciplines, believing that he would ultimately have killed himself if he had continued his slavish commitment to prayers, vigils, reading, fasting, and other exercises of discipline.

Some would try to argue that Isaiah and the Lord himself spoke against practices such as fasting and rituals of worship (Isaiah 58, 59; Matthew 23). In reality, both were speaking out not against the *habit* of fasting but against the *abuse* of the disciplines. So fasting in an attempt to manipulate God, or impress others, is wrong. But Jesus was not writing off the disciplines – he was seeking to protect their integrity.

Put most simply, your prayer life – and mine – will only be what we choose it to be. Maturity in prayer will not mug us in our sleep, blossom as the result of our being in some "special" meeting or service, or grow in any way without our making conscious, realistic, and specific choices on a daily basis. There's no short cut behind our will.

Psychiatrist M. Scott Peck observes:

> There are many people I know who possess a
> vision of personal evolution yet seem to lack the
> will for it. They want, and believe it is possible, to

skip over the discipline, to find an easy shortcut
to sainthood. Often they attempt to attain it by
simply imitating the superficialities of saints,
retiring to the desert or taking up carpentry. Some
even believe that by such imitation they have really
become saints and prophets, and are unable to
acknowledge that they are still children and face the
painful fact that they must start at the beginning
and go through the middle.[5]

And so, while we don't want to get enslaved in legalistic
asceticism, we must face the fact that choice, will, and
discipline are essential ingredients if we are to move further
down the pathway of prayer.

Stephen Travis laments our lack in this area:

In the modern church, qualities such as
perseverance and loyalty are in short supply. In an
age of instant coffee, and instant glue... we don't
take easily to the pain of sticking to unglamorous
tasks, or developing a discipline in prayer. But as
Samuel Chadwick said, "All God's things are grown
things. He is never in the ready-made business."[6]

For me, the choices begin at the beginning of each day in
the shower. Feeling like a drenched corpse, and drifting into
the level of consciousness required in order to negotiate yet

---

5   M. Scott Peck, *The Road Less Travelled*, London: Arrow, 1990. Reprinted
with the permission of Simon & Schuster, Inc. from The Road Less Travelled by
M. Scott Peck, M.D.. Copyright © 1978 M. Scott Peck.
6   Stephen Travis, *You've Got Mail*, Carlisle: Spring Harvest/Authentic, 2002,
p. 34.

another full day of existence on planet Earth, I have to decide: will I begin this day by rushing to the computer to check my email – or will I climb onto my exercise bike, pick up my Bible and sometimes my prayer book as I pedal my way to nowhere? Of course, the former takes no effort at all. Discipline is the bridge to a tended, manicured, cared for life.

Passion and simplicity

Richard Foster, that masterful writer on prayer and discipline, came as a big shock to me when I met him personally. I had expected a measured, serious sage, a modern-day saint of few words and fewer smiles. He is the opposite: Foster is a man who is deeply in love with God and who exudes a sense of fun, relaxation, and occasional hilarity. He writes movingly about the simplicity of prayer:

> We may have been taught that prayer is a sublime and otherworldly activity; that in prayer we are to talk to God *about* God. As a result we are inclined to view our experiences as distractions and intrusions into proper prayer. This is an ethereal, decarnate spirituality. We, on the other hand, worship a God who was born in a smelly stable, who walked this earth in blood, sweat, and tears, but who nevertheless lived in perpetual responsiveness to the heavenly Monitor.
> And so I urge you: carry on an ongoing conversation with God about the daily stuff of life,

a little like Tevye in *Fiddler on the Roof.* For now, do
not worry about 'proper' praying, just talk to God.
Share your hurts; share your sorrows; share your
joys – freely and openly. God listens in compassion
and love, just as we do when our children come to
us. He delights in our presence.[7]

I'm nervous about the complicating of spirituality. Jesus
calls for simple, get-to-the-point praying rather than
cleverly embroidered speech-making. Sometimes there's
only one word that we can say, and it's the only word we
need to say: "Father".

I have sat through too many occasions of public
prayer when I couldn't help wondering who was actually
being addressed. Was this finely manicured speech I could
hear intended for heaven's ear, or was it a work of oratory
designed to impress human ears? That's not to say that a
public prayer can't be a stirring tapestry of oratory, peppered
with biblical truth. But when we take that as our model
for private prayer, we end up with a relationship based on
speeches: hardly a recipe for intimacy. The Lord's Prayer is
profound in its simplicity: we do well to emulate it.

Moment by moment…

Walking through shared experiences develops intimacy.
That's one reason why I don't do well when I'm alone. No
matter how beautiful the sunset, it pales if I cannot celebrate

7   Richard Foster, *Prayer: Finding the Heart's True Home*, London: Hodder &
Stoughton, 1992

its splendour with somebody. Over the last couple of decades my wife Kay and I have spent many holidays with Chris and Jeanne Edwardson, friends from Oregon. One of the many reasons why we love spending time together is their practice of celebrating and being grateful for the fun that we're having together: our conversations are peppered with comments such as "Isn't this great? It doesn't get much better than this, does it?"

Shared experiences aren't limited to those special sunset moments: the chatter of everyday life can be a building block of human relationship. Friendships that demand that no "small" talk be permitted, and that sharing can only be centred around the important, the significant, and the sublime, wear me out. Sometimes we all want to talk small stuff. I believe that the same is true in prayer. We need to learn to chatter with God, who apparently is never bored by our "prattle".

Trying to talk to God in the thirty-minute slot so especially prescribed, without any ongoing conversation during the day, will produce a stilted, awkward praying. I say again: chatter on. He loves it.

Realistic goals in prayer

As we come to the end of this chapter, I want to encourage you to make some goals that are realistic and achievable in your relationship with God. If you're anything like me, you pop off to some prayer conference and the result is that you pledge to pray for countless hours of every day, arising at some impossible time in the morning. Of course, it doesn't happen, but we feel that anything less than a huge commitment is, well, so unworthy.

I hinted at this earlier in the chapter, but let's return to this little discussion of this odd practice of *fantasy commitment*. We feel that to determine to pray for two hours seems appropriate – far more so than a determination to set aside five minutes of quietness and reflection. We thus enter a land of noble aspirations – that result in nothing. Realized objectives are better than noble myths. And it's not only in the realm of prayer that fantasy commitment manifests itself. I could take you to churches where Christians get moved in missionary services and offer themselves to travel to far-flung places in the world, but if you asked them to move from the pew that they occupy every Sunday to another part of the building, or to tell the chap who lives next door about Jesus, there'd be a rebellion. It's easier to believe that I would win thousands to Christ were I to be a missionary than it is to invite the family next door over for dinner. Thus our commitment remains in the fantasyland of our minds. So go ahead – get radical. Make a five-minute appointment with God sometime during today. It could well be the first step towards praying as you can and not praying as you can't.

4

The power of shared prayer

"Say, Our Father…"

"What life have you if you have not life together?"

– T. S. Eliot

When Jesus taught his friends to pray *"Our* Father", he confronted the myth that solitary prayer is the only or best way to pray, and that we don't need the mutuality and strength that comes from being part of a community of prayer – the church. Put most simply, prayer with others is easier. It's a relief to surrender to the truth that, when it comes to spirituality, we really do need each other – we need church; this is by design. But I am nervous, lest we shrink the church down to being merely a support group for little us. Some treat the church with a consumer attitude that reduces it to being nothing more than a feeding centre designed to keep them warm. When the service – literally – is not to their liking or taste, they move on, the "Lord having told us to leave". Such an attitude dwarfs and minimizes the church. Let's pan the camera out to a wider screen view for a few moments, to see that the praying church is more than a blessing club. It is God's gift to a lonely planet. The church is the beacon community, launched with the sending of Abraham, following the disastrous clamouring for a "big society" that excluded God: the tower of Babel. The invitation to come in from the cold, in a culture of arctic techno-isolation, is God's loving call for shivering humanity. But the fireside will only be warm in a church that knows how to engage with God in worship and prayer.

We must reaffirm the value of church, lest we, in our culture obsessed with the personal, end up with no coherent doctrine or understanding of the church at all. Church can rankle: she irritates us, slows us down, winds us up, and seems to defy even the costliest and most energy-sapping attempts to make her more effective. Billions are invested in her annually, but in some parts of the world she is shrinking, despite all of the cash injection. If she were a corporation, her end-of-year results would mean that they'd fire the managing director. At times she seems more like a withered, ugly crone than a blushing bride. We look back with pride at some of her historic exploits: slaves freed, nations reached, freedoms won, the oppressed and marginalized released and included. But we peer over our shoulders and weep with shame too: the screams reverberate from the inquisitor's rack. We lower our heads at the political shenanigans and power struggles, the bloodletting of the Crusades by warriors who went into battle with the sign of the cross emblazoned on their chests. The church has a chequered history.

But she is still one of God's finest ideas – perhaps that in itself, while not excusing her, helps us to understand why she has so often been the object of satanic hijacking throughout history. She is the appointed one, ordained to live a beautiful life and yell back an answer to the orphan culture that is every generation: "You are loved! You are loved!" And never was there a time when the gentle yet firm voice of a praying, Jesus-centred church was more needed.

Techno-isolation is a defining characteristic of our culture: we have ever more efficient methods of hyper-fast communication, and yet with all our gadgets and gizmos, people are still hungry for the warmth of community and friendship. Rapid change, household fragmentation, and increased mobility are all helping to make loneliness the epidemic of the third millennium. For some, the most time-consuming intimate relationship they have is with a computer chip. But try as we might, we still need relationship and community.

The most popular "soaps" on British television are all centred on the dynamics of life, sometimes mundane life in community. In the UK, consider the huge popularity of *EastEnders, Coronation Street, Neighbours, Home and Away*, and more. Their characters are often adulterous and sometimes murderous scoundrels, and yet they are people *together*. Be it in the Rovers' Return, the Queen Vic, or an Australian suburb, these people gravitate around a centrality that is community.

And now, if all those soaps were not enough, we have the media smash hit of the early third millennium: reality television. Who would have thought that *Big Brother* would stand a chance of success? Plant a group of ordinary people in a camera-riddled house for weeks on end, film their every waking – and sleeping – moment, and give them unexciting and mundane tasks to do. I wonder how well that proposal was first received when it surfaced in a television boardroom? Millions have been hooked.

The docu-soap provides us with helpful insights concerning the daily experiences of an airport cleaner – a valuable job, but who would ever have thought it to be the stuff of television? Extreme reality shows such as *Survivor* or *I'm a Celebrity – Get Me Out of Here* give us the chance to see what happens in relationships under extreme conditions. Social networking provides opportunity for interaction and relationship – but still there is a famine of real, face-to-face relationship. And the loneliness carries a high price. Half a million different types of support group (such as Alcoholics Anonymous) exist in the USA.

What does all this scream at us? The missing ingredient in today's Britain is relationships. And when the church takes notice of this, she wins.

The phenomenal impact of Alpha, which is a relational, interactive method of exploring the claims of Christ, testifies to this truth. But think again about Alpha: it is more than a yuppie supper club with a dose of God stuff sprinkled on the dessert, more than a series of lectures with food. With its insistence on emphasizing encounters with God through the

Holy Spirit, Alpha has at its heart a call to intimacy with God, love discovered not only through information but through encounter with the Living God. Our culture is more than lonely and techno-isolated: it is estranged from God. Britain needs more than social club churches; the urgent call is for fun, dynamic, human, relevant, *spiritual* communities that gather together around God. Churches that are, as Dallas Willard says, "communities of prayerful love".

Donald Baillie provides a memorable image of what has gone wrong in our culture, in his insistence that the plan of redemption is the great "tale of God calling his human children to form a great circle for the playing of his game":

> In that circle we ought all to be standing, linked together with lovingly joined hands, facing towards the Light in the centre, which is God ("the Love that moves the sun and the other stars"); seeing our fellow creatures all round the circle in the light of that central Love, which shines on them and beautifies their faces; and joining with them in the dance of God's great game, the rhythm of love universal. But instead of that, we have, each one, turned our backs upon God and the circle of our fellows, and faced the other way, so that we can see neither the Light at the centre nor the faces on the circumference. And indeed in that position it is difficult even to join hands with our fellows! Therefore instead of playing God's game we play, each one, our own selfish little game... Each one of us wishes to be the centre, and there is blind confusion, and

not even any true knowledge of God or of our neighbours. That is what is wrong.[8]

I remember with gratitude the day that I first bumped into a small band of people who were playing God's game.

Happy day

To be blunt, they were quite an odd-looking group, or so I thought.

They sat in a circle, on a mixture of threadbare armchairs and even old settees that had been thoughtfully "donated" to the church. The room where they sat was called "the Minor hall". This room was reserved for after-church cups of tea, plates of biscuits, and – on this occasion – the Sunday night "afterglow". This strangely named event was not, as I feared, a time of ritually sacrificing the old ladies ("Come on then, lads, let's chuck Sister Doris on the fire: she'll burn…") but an informal time of sipping PG Tips, singing, and telling each other about what God had been up to in the previous week. Looking back, it was all wonderful, but this was my first time in the church, and I was nervous, slightly terrified even. I scanned their faces anxiously. Some had their eyes glued shut, their features a mask of worshipful concentration, their hands held aloft. I pondered the meaning of their devotion. Others sat back in their tatty chairs, relaxed, eyes opened: no intensity for them, just relaxing and enjoying the atmosphere of togetherness. A guitarist strummed a few

---

8   Donald Baillie, quoted in Travis, *You've Got Mail*.

chords, and I noticed that he didn't seem to be performing for anyone. He didn't look round to the group for approval of his playing; in fact, he moved through the chord changes with his eyes closed too.

Even the song was odd.

Great is the Lord, and greatly to be praised,
In the city of our God, in the mountain of his holiness.
Beautiful for situation, the joy of the whole earth,
Is Mount Zion, on the sides of the North, the city of the
      great King.

Yikes! What lyrics were these? What in the name of reason was all that "Is Mount Zion on the sides of the North?" stuff? Were they asking for directions? If so, why sing the request to each other? It was, as Alice would say, "Curiouser and curiouser…"

I watched them, initially standing by the door, too afraid to join their circle, but strangely aware that they had something that was way beyond my grasp.

The song ended, and the kettle had come to the boil, and so "the time of fellowship" began. I couldn't escape now – and anyway, I realized with some alarm, I didn't want to. One after another, without making me some kind of embarrassed centre of attention, they came and shook my hand and smiled and murmured that they were glad that I was there, and the weirdest thing of all – I knew that they really were glad. When they asked me what I had thought about the earlier evening service, I didn't feel interrogated.

They all knew that I wasn't a Christian, but nobody selected me for a good gospel thrashing. No one attempted to ram anything down my throat; they seemed real, honest – and they were big on God. Within an hour I found myself quietly kneeling to begin the nearly forty-year-old journey as a Christian that continues today. And then they formed a long line – literally – that went all the way to the back of the building as they delightedly welcomed me into the family of God.

I had found a loving church – and I will always be in their debt. In the coming months those people listened to my ridiculous questions – but never made me feel small. They didn't tut-tut when I used the contents page of my Bible, even though they could flip right to the portion of Scripture they wanted with precision and ease. I was carless, and they gave me lifts to and from church, even when it was very late. They took me out for pizza and treated me as if I were a lifelong friend. And when they sensed that I was messing up in my personal behaviour, they didn't lecture or scold or give me a haughty glare, but gently, kindly guided me as I allowed them to. Yes, I had found a loving church. Looking back, some of the songs that we sang were pretty cheesy. Not everything was right, and with church it never is.

But I came to love God because of them, and I began a romance with his church as well. I'm uncomfortable around the cynics who seem to love to celebrate the weaknesses of the church. For me, it was and is a community that welcomed me in from the cold; that church spoke hope and life into my troubled young heart and became a genuine family to me. God is head over heels in love with the church; certainly, it's flawed, but it can be very beautiful. Nearly forty years ago I got a first-hand taste of its glory.

I hadn't been back to that rusty old tin building for years, but, passing through the town, I decided to stop by on the off chance that someone might be in there. I knocked on the door, and the young man turned older who had strummed that guitar so many years earlier opened it. Initially he didn't recognize me – time has not been that kind in my case – but once I introduced myself, I was greeted once again with a big, wide smile and open arms.

I wandered back into the Minor Hall. The old chairs were long gone – and many of the people who had sat in them on that long-lost night of my youth were no longer to be seen. But it felt like a holy moment as I stood quietly, alone for a while, and remembered their songs, their kindness, and their love.

I'll always be grateful that I bumped into a loving church. Grateful for ever. Literally.

Prayer at the heart of the game

What was it about those people that was so magnetic and inviting? As I said, they were certainly kind and welcoming, but there was a special, deeper something about them. I am convinced that I was compelled by their sense of devotion to Jesus. They seemed to be good people, but there was more than sterile purity and cold morality. They enjoyed one another's company, but they were more than a good club to join. And as for their style – frankly, it was alien to me. But I found them compelling because they were a diverse group of people who shared a common love; their spirituality was arresting and real. I had caught a whiff of what Keith Miller calls "the scent of love". It was an intoxicating, heady fragrance.

> The early Church grew not because of the spiritual gifts of Christians such as the gift of speaking in tongues and not because Christianity was such a palatable doctrine (to the contrary, it is about the most unpalatable doctrine there is) but because they had discovered the secret of community. Generally they did not have to lift a finger to evangelize. Someone would be walking down a back alley in Corinth or Ephesus and would see a group of people sitting together talking about the strangest things – something about a man and a tree and an execution and an empty tomb. What they were talking about made no sense to the onlooker. But there was something about the way they spoke to one another, about the way they looked at one another, about the way they cried together, the way they laughed together, the way they touched one another that was strangely appealing. It gave off the scent of love. The onlooker would start to drift farther down the alley, only to be pulled back to this little group like a bee to a flower. He would listen some more, still not

understanding, and start to drift away again. But
again he would be pulled back, thinking, I don't
have the slightest idea what these people are talking
about, but whatever it is, I want part of it.[9]

I certainly wanted a part of it that night. Nearly forty years
later, I still do. And I am convinced that the greatest need
in the world today is for a church that is at ease with prayer,
but also at ease with each other. Nothing else will really do.
The church that has not learned to be together with Jesus
in the place of prayer may be adept at changing the social
conditions of its community for the better. But if spirituality
is not at the heart of social action, it is diluted into a vague
do-goodism that leads to little. For sure, people's lives are
made better, but the *reason* for the improvement lies beyond
their grasp; they fail to see that it is because of the love of God
that life has improved. Their environment might be better,
but their hearts remain unmoved and unreached. That is not
to say that all social action needs to lead to evangelism, be
badged "for Jesus' sake", or exclude partnership with people
of other faiths or none. On the contrary. But warm faith and
friendship with God must sit at the heart of who we are.

The church that does not centre itself in prayer will
turn passionate evangelism into cold expansionism at best
(church growth for its own sake) and, at worst, will stop
sharing the good news with clarity and passion altogether.
Distance from the heartbeat of God will cause a gradual
erosion of enthusiasm for mission. At first the shift will
be slow, and almost imperceptible. Only after a few years

---

9   Reprinted by permission. *The Scent of Love*, Keith Miller, 1983, Thomas
Nelson Inc. Nashville, Tennessee. All rights reserved.

will some pause, look back, and ask the haunting question: whatever happened to mission and evangelism? Why do we no longer know the joy and mess of having brand new Christians around? And new Christians are the lifeblood of the church, its *raison d'être*.

The church that does not centre its action and activities around prayer will eventually be driven more by market forces and consumer demands than the heart and intentions of God. Its services and meetings will dispense good, orthodox information *about* God, but there will be few opportunities for the theory to become reality. Indeed, many churches become little more than carefully designed mechanisms that are actually constructed to keep God at a healthy distance. A theology of the immanence of God may be part of their orthodoxy, but the suggestion that God might actually do anything other than speak through the pages of the preached Bible is met with corporately raised eyebrows of deep suspicion.

We must learn and hold on to the joy of whispering and shouting, "Our Father" together.

The disciplines of silence and solitude are being rediscovered as we search for a coherent spirituality, but let's not emphasize them at the expense of community devotion.

> In the past standardized congregations required everyone to sit, stand and kneel at the same time. They were instructed what to think through the sermon, and it was expected that they would all believe roughly the same. People who did not fit

the mould left. The evacuation of the church since the 1950s involved a flight from this uniform approach.

Some people have taken refuge in highly individualistic forms of spirituality, spirituality that is practised in groups of one. But it is not easy for spirituality to flourish when you are on your own. It can help to pray with other people, whether the prayers are formal, extempore or silent. A group in prayer creates an atmosphere, which encourages each member to pray. Being with others aids worship too. As other people come into the presence of God you are drawn along with them. Learning about the faith with others provides stimulation and encouragement. The larger entity creates a context in which the individual can encounter God. Take away that context, and it becomes harder to develop your spirituality… while there is certainly a place for personal prayer and study, there is little future for solo-spirituality done purely on your own.[10]

But isn't prayer supposed to be private?

Some would like us to believe that Jesus taught "solo-spirituality" as the only legitimate expression of prayer, and they reject the idea of public prayer gatherings or a call to collective fasting. Certainly the Sermon on the Mount was a

10 Michael Moynagh, *Changing World, Changing Church*, London: Monarch, 2001.

clear slap in the face for the blow-your-own-trumpet religious contortions employed by the Pharisees. And the Pharisees were big on outward show. They dressed to make a religious fashion statement, adorning themselves with tephillin (small leather boxes containing portions of Scripture) and tassels (the four tassels from the prayer shawl). The message was screamingly obvious: "Hello, everyone, look at me, listen to me: I pray, I give…"

We do know that there was a small area in the Temple – hidden away – called the Chamber of the Silent. It was there that the embarrassed poor could go for help without the identity of the helper ever being revealed. But the problem was not with the public *context* of the Pharisees' prayer and fasting – it was the smug, self-preening *attitude* with which they entered the public arena that provoked Jesus to open fire.

If public spirituality is forbidden, then Jesus broke his own guidelines with a ministry of the miraculous that was so blatantly in the public arena; and the early church, in their corporate gatherings, misunderstood him too. What Jesus is talking about in the Great Sermon is the pride that strikes when the public is about – the obsession with being noticed.

Gerard Kelly sums up this peacock-preening piety incisively:

> *Some pray like a BMW:*
> *Seven coats*
> *of shine and shimmer*
> *masking*

the hardness of steel,
with an anti-emotion warranty
to guard against
the least sign of trust.

Some pray like a Porsche:
nought to victory
in 6.7 seconds,
banking on the promises
of pray-as-you-earn prosperity.

Jesus recommended praying
in the garage
with the door shut
and the radio off,
praying when no one is looking,
forgetting
the traffic of the day,
preferring the quiet lay-by
to the clamour
of the Pray and Display.[11]

Naturally supernatural

One of the best ways to develop a corporate atmosphere of prayer together without falling into the trap of prideful piety is to develop a natural feel to our praying. Prayer that

11 "The Games People Pray", in Gerard Kelly, *Spoken Worship*, Grand Rapids: Zondervan, 2007, p. 37. Used with permission of the author.

is conversational, simple, that does not invoke a drum roll – or a roll of the eyes – or say, "Oh, gosh, we're *really* godly, aren't we?" is the prayer that pleases God and keeps us away from deadly Pharisaism. We should be able to walk down the street together and ease into a conversation with God in a way that doesn't suggest that we've either lost our sanity or obtained a PhD in religiosity.

Develop a culture of gratitude in your church and your friendships – and not just for food. And on the subject of "saying grace", avoid the subtle trap of being religiously non-religious. I know people who have rejected the practice of giving thanks before eating together because it can descend into a hurried mantra that actually is irritating. The food gets cold and the wooden prayer is just a monotonous litany that contains a momentary nodding awareness that there are millions who won't eat today. But those who react against this, in their insistence that religious rituals can lose any sense of reality and heart, now religiously *don't* say grace, and are appalled at anyone who does. "Say grace? Are you serious?" A new religious habit has been formed around what we *don't* do.

Give yourselves to *seasons* of special prayer in your church. Find a prayer partner, or get into a prayer friendship group. Years ago, friends of mine formed a prayer cell that met weekly on the South Downs of England to pray for West Sussex. Rain, shine, or icy snow, they were up on those draughty hills faithfully every week. They concluded their evening of prayer by heading down to a local pub in the village and enjoying a couple of beers. When I visited the pub, the landlord had no idea that I knew them or that I was a Christian. Pulling me a pint, he nodded over at the group in the corner. "See those blokes over there, mate? They're Christians, you know…" I braced myself for the expected oh-what-a-bunch-of-drips-and-they're-hypocrites-too speech. It never came. His face a broad smile, the landlord continued. "Every Monday night, whatever the weather, they go up on the hills to pray for Chichester. Marvellous, isn't it? The whole village knows who they are." I spent a few happy evenings by the log fire in that pub participating in chats that the whole bar was a part of – conversations that included God, the gospel, the church – without awkwardness or embarrassment.

The awesome power of agreement

Dallas Willard points out that the church is a community with *request* at its heart: we are people who have been appointed by God to petition him together. Through Christ we have been granted the privilege and confidence to be a requesting people.

When we learn to agree together, we bring the filter of community to our requests; we can check and confront each other, and prevent the meandering up selfish back roads that can happen when the request is known only inside one head. In agreement we can encourage one another in persistence and tenacity, spurring each other on to continue in the place of request. And we can bear one another's burdens in the place of agreed request, encouraging each other relationally even as we do battle spiritually.

Agreement can bring the generations across the church together too. So often we can be tempted to hive off to our generational stylistic preferences – we gather around our stated worship and music expression, rather than the centrality that we are one in Christ. In a way, we are setting ourselves up for the calamities that visit any church that is consumer-driven.

Change your church

Perhaps you are frustrated right now, a little angry even, because you know that the church of which you are a part does not have natural, heartfelt praying as part of its culture. Avoid the temptation to start talking and thinking about *them*. I notice that when our church does something right, we use the word "we" or "us", happy to align ourselves to the outfit when it's doing well. When weakness is diagnosed, we like to step out of it for a moment, preferring to refer to the group as "they" or "them", distancing ourselves. But the church, in its strengths and weaknesses both, is us. Like it or not, we are contributors individually to what it has become collectively. The *they* people usually become self-righteous scourges of the church, self-appointed pains in everyone's necks – don't do it.

Own responsibility, and seek to bring prayer into your relationships. Some will roll their eyes and think that you are being pretentious – don't feel the need to defend it, or give them a lecture on their own gross carnality! Little by little, the practice of celebration, gratitude, and request can be introduced into the little cultures that we all of us create – and the church changed as a result.

5

The alphabet of prayer begins with F for Father

"Our Father…"

"If you want to judge how well a person understands Christianity, find out how much they make of the thought of being God's child, and having God as their Father. If this is not the thought that prompts and controls their worship and prayers and their whole outlook on life, it means that they do not understand Christianity very well."

– Jim Packer[12]

My dog thinks that I'm the Antichrist. He's called Arnie, named after Arnold Schwarzenegger. It seemed like a good idea at the time. He has a chocolate-box face that melts most

---

12 J. I. Packer, *Knowing God*, Downers Grove: IVP, 1993, pp. 201–202.

hearts, and the straggly, floppy ears gifted to all Cavalier King Charles Spaniels, and he views me with the affection that one might feel for a serial killer. So why this sniff of disdain, this haughty, silent rejection treatment that cats are expert at but dogs emulate quite well? After all, I've taken him for at least ten walks in the last five years (don't alert the RSPCA – we lash him to a treadmill every morning: *not really*). And I am occasionally the one who opens the huge sack of beef-scented rabbit droppings that constitutes his food supply. Still he hates me.

I've managed to work out why I am so low in Arnie's pecking – or barking – order. It's all about *negative expectation*. He has instinctively established that a telling-off is inevitable when I'm around. I'm always the one who tells him to get down when he jumps up at the legs of our guests when they come into our home. It seems to me that one should be able to visit friends without having a furry black snout snuffling all over you. So I tell him off. He obediently desists, and then settles himself down on the feet of the now seated guest, as if to say, "I don't know you at all, but I really like you. But as for *him…*" If dogs could spit, mine would.

And so, whenever I call his name, he gets up and walks woodenly to his basket. It doesn't matter if I make ridiculous cooing noises, click my fingers in welcome, purse my lips in a friendly whistle, or even sit there gently toying with a five-pound slab of steak. Arnie hears my voice, and has convinced himself that the sound of it is an overture for a telling-off. Off he goes, my warmest offer of fuss and affection rejected again.

Forgive the illustration from the friendship (or lack of same) betwixt my dog and me, but I want to use it to provide a backdrop for our look at a few more myths about prayer. The issue, once again, is that of negative expectation. Some of us don't bother even to try to spend time with God, because we're convinced that the possibility that he might say something to us probably means that we're going to get a good telling-off. Surely the One who is ablaze in awesome holiness couldn't say anything other than "Could do better"? Prayer inevitably becomes a chore, because it is viewed as a frosty chat with a snooty headmaster who is bound to mark our test papers by scrawling a huge "F" all over our lives.

There are plenty of people who think that God is a never-pleased taskmaster. It's reported that John Cleese recently confessed that he'd love to be a Christian, but he couldn't pass the exam. But this is the gospel reversed. Yes, God can be hugely demanding. But he is also the One who, while pointing out the weaknesses of the seven churches in the book of Revelation, was also able to commend some of them with a hearty "Well done." Some of them had worked hard, pursued truth, and stayed faithful in suffering. The risen Jesus congratulated them for it.

If we're ever going to get deeper into prayer, we must first realize that an encounter with God does not necessarily mean that it's another bad news, "Get in your basket" type of meeting. Can we believe in the possibility of heaven's congratulations and affection, the promise of the One who calls himself Love? We are welcomed people. This answers the great enquiry of lonely humanity.

Knowing love

The nagging question that gnaws away inside each and every one of us is, "Do you love me?" It fuels much or even most of the activity that we call life. The question waits quietly in the wings, prompting a persistent, aching longing. Are we loved?

> The joint, as Fats Waller would have said, was jumping… And, during the last set, the saxophone player took off on a terrific solo. He was a kid from some insane place like Jersey City or Syracuse, but somewhere along the line he had discovered he could say it with a saxophone. He stood there, wide-legged, humping the air, filling his barrel chest, shivering in the rags of his twenty-odd years, and screaming through the horn, '*Do you love me?*' '*Do you love me?*' '*Do you love me?*' And again, '*Do you love me?*' '*Do you love me?*' '*Do you love me?*' The same phrase unbearable, endlessly and variously repeated with all the force the boy had… the question was terrible and real. The boy was blowing with his lungs and guts out of his own short past; somewhere in the past in gutters or gang fights… in the acrid room, behind marijuana or the needle, under the smell in the precinct basement, he had received a blow from which he would never recover, and this no one wanted to believe. *Do you love me? Do you love me? Do you love me?* The men on the stand stayed with him cool and at a little distance, adding and questioning. But each man knew that the boy was blowing for everyone of them…[13]

13   James Baldwin, *Another Country*, New York: The Dial Press, 1962.

There is a sure answer to the agonizing query, and it is a definite yes. But how can we humans, stumbling and fumbling around in the dark as we are, know that love? We may hear that there is a God whose name and primary identity is love, but where are the tokens and expressions of his love to be found? We can catch a whisper of romance from creation. Extravagant sunsets seem to carry the signature of a loving artist who nightly signs off the day with the flourish of a fluorescent pen. Towering mountains point towards more than cold design, and boom the deep bass resonance of solid, dependable love. The fingerprint of the Lover is clearly stamped across everything that he has made. And yet we all sometimes wonder: is all of this just wishful thinking? We need a clearer message, a more certain herald of love. Thankfully, God has *demonstrated* his love in the giving of his Son, and *described* that love in the Scriptures. And he has planned that his church be a *working model* of lives lived in tune with the symphony of that love.

In the inspiration of his word, God apparently likes to use superlatives, to write his love notes in arresting language. He employs them repeatedly throughout the New Testament to let us know just how valuable we are to him. There we are lovingly told that we belong to a royal priesthood, we're the honoured citizens of a new, holy nation. We are a people who belong to God, his prized, delightful possessions. We are uniquely God's workmanship. Why the shower of superlatives? Certainly the Lord is not in the habit of throwing cheesy platitudes about like a heavenly greeting card writer, in an attempt to cheer us up for a second or two. He is in the serious business of letting us know that we're priceless. God is not into mere precious moments and superficial backslapping. We are greatly loved.

But we find it difficult to believe that all this wonderful news – good news indeed – is actually true of *us*. We are prepared to nod in mental assent to the idea that God generically loves his church, and we concede that there are other, far more Christianly people than us out there that are the apple of Jesus' eye. But not us. No, we who are treated to a relatively uninterrupted view of the mucky dungeons of our inner lives can never feel that our cold cells could echo with the footstep of the Great Lover coming to *us*. Mother Teresa maybe, and all those ancient devotional types whom we met briefly earlier, who dressed in hair shirts, drew blood with pious whipping, and refused to wash because of the pleasure of water cleansing the skin. They were keen enough to merit love. And maybe old Mrs Smith who wears her fingers to the bone knitting psychedelic tea cosies for distant sweating missionaries – yes, she must be loved, what with all that knit-one-purl-one-knit-one-purl-one for Jesus down through the years. And that slightly odd chap who *always* raises his hands during the worship – and the notices too – he's *really* keen. But me? Not likely.

I have experimented with this theory of mass self-rejection that is prevalent – epidemic, even – among Christians. March into a large meeting, take upon yourself a glazed-eyed, prophet-at-large look, and announce in thunderous tones that God has hereby spoken with you while on the way to the service, and that he has revealed unto yourself the *specific identity (first and last names, and also the colour of their front doors)* of some parishioners present who have been guilty of GREAT NAUGHTINESS – shout loud enough – and watch everyone duck. When it's time to call up volunteers for the death row of public judgment, most of us live with a lingering suspicion that *our* name is the next one to be called. Christians line up with the downcast recognition that they are surely to trudge the Green Mile of shame.

Try the same procedure in reverse. Soften your voice, allow a warm glaze to come over your eyes, and announce that God has let you know the identities of some people present who he hereby says are *wonderful, fantastic, faithful, glorious, lovely disciples of his.* Check out the audience. None of them are ducking, fearful; no whitened knuckles grip the pews now. No, everyone is peering around the place trying to figure out who on earth these divine bouquets are being delivered to. And most people think that the flowers can't possibly be for them. How can he really love me?

A friend who is going through a turbulent time emailed me just this morning. With permission, I share her painful dilemma:

> Have you ever wondered if you were really saved?
> The thought occurred to me in the middle of last
> Sunday's service. I cannot believe for myself that
> God really loves me as I am. I can believe it for
> others but I can't seem to grasp this ever-important
> teaching. So the thought was: if you can't believe
> the whole thing, how can you only believe part

of it and still be OK? And do you think God is
punishing me for these thoughts? Just look at me.
My marriage is hanging by a thread; what kind of
mother would have a screaming child, and what
kind of pastor's wife would end up doing time in a
mental ward? Is this redeemable? And do we really
have to do Christmas this year?

A missionary – and missionaries are obviously known for
their high levels of commitment to and sacrifices for Jesus
– wrote of her lingering feeling that the God who loves the
world might stop short of liking her:

> Our inability to develop a truly God-shaped set of
> expectations easily could leave us wandering out
> the forty years or so of our adult lives in our own
> self-made desert wilderness. In my case, the greatest
> consequence of long-term, misplaced expectations
> has been their deadening effect on spiritual vitality.
> I questioned God, myself, my circumstances…
> God must not love me the way He loves others, I
> thought. I must be on Jesus' blacklist. I guess I'm
> just one of those Christians that God can't use.[14]

All of this obviously has devastating effects on our ability to
pray. Why would we even bother to try to draw near to the
One who we are sure will reject us? Some of us don't pray
because we don't feel welcome, and we couldn't be more
wrong. When Jesus taught his disciples to say "Our Father",
he was not just laying out a protocol for entry into the

---

14 Carol Kent, *Secret Longings of the Heart*, Colorado Springs: NavPress, 1990.

divine presence, or an opportunity for us to let God know who he is. "Our Father" lets *us* know who God is. And Jesus' teaching on this was not without cost, as radical as it is. The pagans used to address God as father, but Jews were not in that general habit, mainly because the fatherhood of God is not a central theme in Old Testament biblical theology. And so Jewish prayers would focus on the multiple titles of sovereignty, and the Lordship, glory, and grace of God; it must have seemed outrageous to hear Jesus and his disciples talking about God as Father. But he insists that we know we are welcome. For some, this seems just too good to be true.

Good good news

Most of us have been taught a philosophy of suspicion: "If the deal looks too good to be true, then it probably *isn't* true… There's no such thing as a free lunch… Everyone has to pay their own way," and even the oft-quoted but utterly unbiblical "God helps those who help themselves."

As children, those of us who were blessed enough to be raised in a positive, safe environment are most likely to be at ease with the idea of grace and receiving gifts. I know that my children never protested when they were given a chocolate bar, never exhibited any concern that perhaps they might be unworthy of the gift. They were not in the habit of asking me if I had made the mortgage payment that month, or to confirm that I could afford to give them the aforementioned confectionery. As children, their hearts were not cluttered with inhibitions about receiving. Without a further word, the chocolate disappeared down their throats at the speed of light.

But the dawning of adulthood and so-called "maturity" can bring with it the death of our ability to receive easily. Our coming of age can signal the end of many great attributes of childhood, such as innocence, hope, play, adventure, and imagination. Our sense of ease when we are the recipients of gifts can shrivel as the years pile up too. Try giving a gift to some people when (a) it's not Christmas or their birthday – and therefore is not anticipated or expected, and (b) when they have no opportunity to give you something back – and therefore the generosity cannot be reciprocated. You may find yourself observing a major crisis. "You shouldn't have. I don't know what to say. I didn't get you anything. I feel *so* embarrassed."

There have been millions of Christians who have operated their whole lives in this sense of embarrassed crisis when it comes to the freely given grace of God. So they stay out in the cold, shivering strangers to the wild welcome party that the Father throws for us all, if we will only come inside.

The early church fathers could hardly believe this concept of fatherhood. It seemed too good a deal to be true. They added a nervous preface to the Lord's Prayer, a hesitant peek around the corner to see if it was OK to run into the arms of God. "Grant that we may dare to call on Thee as Father" was their prayer. It was as if they were saying, "Can we really do this?"

They were wrong in their hesitancy, but perhaps entirely

right in the addition, sensing as they did the hesitation that flutters in most human hearts when they are invited to call him Father. But the alphabet of Christianity starts with F for Father – not failure. Many Christians today – leaders included – wrestle with the stunning idea that heaven's courts might roll out a red carpet of welcome for *them*. No wonder prayer is not frequently associated with laughter – or joy of any kind. And when that is our lot, we will be more at home with tears of remorse than laughter or fun.

McDonald's intercession: instant agony

I was standing in a minister's office, ready to go into a meeting where I would preach. Everyone looked bright, happy, positive – until someone suggested that we should pray for the service in general and me in particular. What happened in the next three seconds would have provided a wealth of material for a psychological study of Christian spirituality. In an instant, everyone around me burst into tears (there were no actual tears, just the sound of much wailing and crying) as each person came mournfully into the presence of a God who they assumed must be irritated with them. There is of course a time to cry, but this fast-food style of intercessory wailing was disturbing. As soon as the prayer finished, everyone stopped sobbing, brightened up, and began an immediate discussion about the football results. If my children burst into crocodile tears every time they saw me, I'd be worried.

I occasionally visit church buildings where there are "altar benches" or "mourners' benches" placed at the front of the building, purpose-made furniture for penitents, with boxes of tissues thoughtfully provided. I'll concede again that there is certainly a time to weep as well as laugh. Some who come forward for prayer are distressed because they're walking through valley times of serious difficulty or grief, and therefore the tissues are a thoughtful addition. But I am nervous about the implication that to come into the presence of God means that tears are the likely result – unless, of course, we are rediscovering a sense of awe. Now that would be welcome, tears and all.

Missing it: the Father for my perfect future

Some of us live under the deception that *one day* we will be welcome in the presence of God – when we're less sinful, more mature, more accomplished in service. Our welcome is in the future, but the present is blighted with a sense of banishment. It is obvious, yet needs to be said: if we are waiting to be whole before we venture into friendship with the Healer, we will never pray, barred from the courts of God by yet another pervasive myth.

There is a mad irony in the idea that we have to come to God strong and whole, and therefore back off from him because we're not. He is the physician offering a clinic for the sick. In his teaching on prayer, Jesus made an opportunity to seek forgiveness a central and pivotal part of the prayer act, encouraging us to ask that our debts might be forgiven – more on that later. The irony is further compounded by the fact that the more enthusiastic believers are the ones who feel their sinfulness most keenly (their desire to please God is heightened, and their conscience with it), and in their zealous shame they run from the God who gathers the Mephibosheths, those who are invited to the party despite being acutely conscious of their emotional and spiritual disabilities.

Missing it: the Father for my past

Then there's the subtle deception that somehow God *has* loved me in the past alone – that his love rose like a huge wave when Jesus went to the cross to die for my sins, and that there love was poured out, and in a sense, was spent. This locks God's love up in history and turns it into a noble fossil, an emotional antique. Calvary was indeed the crowning work of grace, but it was not a one-hour fleeting wonder, a brief flush of romance. God didn't just love us in terms of an action of the past, he *is and remains* love in his nature and make-up, right this very second. That means that everything he thinks and feels and does is entirely consistent with his primary DNA, which is love. And that means that there is a heart at the core of the universe that beats quickly about you, now. One writer puts it well, and not merely sentimentally: "If God had a refrigerator, your picture would be on it. If God had a wallet, your photo would be in it."[15]

15 Mark Stibbe, *From Orphans to Heirs*, Oxford: Bible Reading Fellowship, 1999.

That is true of the God of today – and of the you that you are today as well. The huge torrent of love that God felt towards you, even at the precise moment of Jesus' death (he knew of you back then, before you were born), is the massive love he feels and has towards you this very second, even as your eyes scan the typeface of these words.

Søren Kierkegaard prays thus:

You have loved us first, O God, alas! We speak of it in terms of history as if You loved us first but a single time, rather than without ceasing. You have loved us first many times and every day and our whole life through. When we wake up in the morning and turn our soul toward you – you are there first – you have loved us first; if I rise at dawn and at the same second turn my soul toward you in prayer, you are there ahead of me, you have loved me first. When I withdraw from the distractions of the day and turn my soul toward you, you are there first and thus forever. And we speak ungratefully as if you have loved us first only once.[16]

Claiming it: grace for *now*

Grace cannot be measured, metered, or contained any more than we can cup the universe in our hands. It is scandalous, abounding, explosive – and, in a sense, dangerous, in that we can misuse it. Perhaps it takes a forgiven slave-owner like

16 Quoted in Richard J. Foster and James Bryan Smith, *Devotional Classics*, San Francisco: Harper, 1993, p. 107.

Newton to be allowed to use the word "amazing".

Consider the mad mathematics of grace…

> People are prepared for everything except for the
> fact that beyond the darkness of their blindness
> there is a great light. They are prepared to go on
> breaking their backs ploughing the same old field
> until the cows come home without seeing, until
> they stub their toes on it, that there is treasure
> buried in that field rich enough to buy Texas.
> They are prepared for a God who strikes hard
> bargains but not for a God who gives as much for
> an hour's work as for a day's. They are prepared for
> a mustard-seed kingdom of God no bigger than
> the eye of a newt but not for the great banyan it
> becomes with birds in its branches singing Mozart.
> They are prepared for the potluck supper at First
> Presbyterian but not for the marriage supper of
> the lamb.[17]

Grace announces the verdict of God that seems like insanity
to our cool, but fundamentally flawed, logic. Philip Yancey
says: "The world thirsts for grace. When grace descends, the
world falls silent before it."[18]

Karl Barth, the world-famous theologian, arrived at
the University of Chicago to deliver some lectures and was
asked by the press what was the most profound truth he
had learned in all his years of study. Barth thought for a

17 Frederick Buechner, *Telling the Truth*, San Francisco: Harper & Row,
1997, p. 70.
18 Philip Yancey, *What's so Amazing About Grace?*, Grand Rapids: Zondervan,
2002, p. 36.

moment, and then responded: "The deepest and most profound truth that I have ever discovered is this: Jesus loves me, this I know, for the Bible tells me so."

But like the Prodigal, wrestling in the hug of his father and desperate to still deliver his "I'm not worthy to be called your son: make me like one of your hired servants" speech, we resist the idea of outrageous grace poured out on *us*. We are the descendants of super-wrestler Jacob, whose prayer was "I will not let you go until you bless me." But our wrestling turns his prayer around on its head. "I will not let you bless me: let me go."

God: not our *natural* father, but adoptive by choice

Mark Stibbe, himself an orphan whose life was wonderfully transformed by an adopting family, has written with warmth and beauty about the biblical truth of adoption. He claims that the struggles of the Reformation wonderfully recovered the great truth of justification by faith, but that this is basically the language of the courtroom. So God is portrayed as judge; a judge appeased. A crime – the sins of humanity – is paid for in full by the shed blood of Christ, but God remains the judge nonetheless. But there is a further lost treasure in the New Testament that leads us, as Stibbe says, "from the language of the courtroom to the language of the family room". This "ultimate blessing of the Gospel" (Jim Packer's description) is the truth that we who are in Christ have been formally adopted into the family of God. God has only one *natural* son – his name is Jesus, and he is and has always been the Son. But now our "big brother" Jesus has laid down his life for us, opening the way for smeared, sinful us also to find a way into the Father's house, not as cringing servants but as sons and daughters. The good Fatherhood of God, the sufferings of his Son and the message of his grace and adopting love must be at the heart of our churches if we are to live with a sense that we are welcomed into his presence – and so can draw near to God's throne with confidence. Stibbe also says that a worship song written some years ago by Ishmael was part of the trigger process that brought him into a new-found sense of God's wonderful adopting love:

> *Father God, I wonder*
> *how I managed to exist*
> *without the knowledge of your parenthood*
> *and your loving care.*
> *Now I am your son,*
> *I am adopted in your family,*
> *And I can never be alone*
> *'Cos Father God you're there beside me.*
>
> *I will sing your praises… for evermore.*[19]

---

19 Extract taken from the song "I Will Sing Your Praises" by Ian Smale. Copyright © 1984 Thankyou Music.

Fatherhood and the prayer experience

Fatherhood is not optional in relationship to our spirituality: Jesus insists in his teaching that we use the language of family when we come to God in prayer. When we approach God, he will not let us be content with addressing him as Lord, King, Sovereign, Creator – or even simply as God. He is, of course, all of the above, and yet insists on being *more* to us than all of these. To come to him as merely God or Lord is to enter into dialogue with him on the basis of his *power* and the extent of his reign – but makes no reference to his *relationship* to us and ours to him. But every single time we use the word "Father" we celebrate and remind ourselves that we are his, and he ours: every prayer becomes another family reunion. And the insistence that we call him Father takes us beyond the God-as-my-vending-machine mechanics that can characterize some praying, and draws us once again, not just to the Potentate of Potentates (though that he surely is) but to a warm bosom of love. He simply will not let us shout our prayers from a distance. Every time we utter his name, we remember that we are home, and that we are his children.

Once our family relationship has been established, our calling him "Father" also reminds us that we come to One who is able to change things – he has the power. He offers us insight from his vantage point: he has the wisdom. As children we are freely invited to bring our requests without hesitation. Again, this flies in the face of our human experience, where we might have been scolded by our human parents because of our incessant begging for yet another chocolate bar or another unneeded toy. Yet we serve a God whose only complaints in this respect seem to be about our *not* asking, or when our asking has an obsessive selfishness at its heart. "When you ask, you do not receive, because you ask with wrong motives, that you may spend what you get on your pleasures" (James 4:3).

The invitation – and command – to come to him as Father establishes a protocol of communication. It should be neither the distant, formal speechmaking that one might use when addressing a king, nor the matey chumminess that one might use with a friend. Our privilege is to know intimacy without flippancy.

Greater expectations

The more time I spend around Christians – and indeed as I delve into the mysterious inner space of my own heart – the more I conclude that most of us have fairly low expectations of what it means to be in friendship with God. We are like the returning Prodigal, who could only hope for a menial job and a square meal from his father's hand. "Make me one of your hired men" was his practised liturgy. And, come to think of it, his logic was reasonable. Hadn't he effectively treated his father as dead when he demanded his inheritance – even though his dad was still alive and well? Hadn't he then turned around and blown the whole lot on a wretched lifestyle that he knew would have broken his father's heart?

Based on the human calculations that we are all surrounded by, logic said that a servant's job would be the *most* that he could anticipate; indeed, he could well be sent packing with an empty stomach and a parental flea in his ear.

But our small thinking about him does not box in God. He has been assaulted and caricatured by our small doctrines, and the result is a perception of a pernickety, mealy-mouthed God who is more like an obsessive-compulsive miser than a wildly generous dad. God has been disguised, his beauty masked. Perhaps that is why Dietrich Bonhoeffer said that the church's main task is to "wash the face of Jesus", to remove the religious grime with which he has been smeared – most often by the church – over the years. The real shining face of Jesus will be, to many, irresistible – if they could only get a glimpse of it.

Robert Farrar Capon wrote:

> The Messiah whom Jesus' contemporaries expected
> – and likewise any and all of the messiahs the world
> has looked to ever since… are like nothing so much
> as the religious version of 'Santa Claus is coming
> to town'. The words of that dreadful Christmas
> song sum up perfectly the only kind of messianic
> behaviour the human race, in its self-destructive
> folly, is prepared to accept: 'He's making a list,
> he's checking it twice, he going to find out who's
> naughty or nice' – and so on into the dark night of
> all the tests this naughty world can ever pass…
>
>   Jesus… is not, thank God, Santa Claus. He
> will come to the world's sins with no list to check,

no tests to grade, no debts to collect, no scores
to settle. He will wipe away the handwriting that
was against us and nail it to his cross (Col. 2:14).
He will save, not some minuscule coterie of good
little boys and girls with religious money in their
piggy banks, but all the stone broke, deadbeat, over
extended children of the world whom He, as the
son of man – the Holy Child of God, the Ultimate
Big kid, if you please – will set free in the liberation
of his death… he tacks a 'Gone Fishing' sign over
the sweatshop of religion, and for all the debts of
all sinners who ever lived, he provided the exact
change for free. How nice it would be if the church
could only remember to keep itself in on the joke.[20]

The Fatherhood of God – it's the basis for our confidence in prayer. It's the celebration message the world is quite literally dying to hear. I like Capon's analogy of the "joke". How wonderful it will be when more of those who are deeply saddened and depressed by Satan's plastic trinkets hear the infectious sound of our salvation laughter.

---

20 Robert Farrar Capon, *The Parables of Grace*, Grand Rapids: Wm. B. Eerdmans, 1988.

6

God is right here, right now

"Who is in the heavens…"

"Some… think that God is a Wizard-of-Oz or Sistine-Chapel kind of being sitting at a location very remote from us."

– Dallas Willard

Jesus teaches us to pray to our Father who is in heaven – but what does that mean? Is God up there, aeons away – while we are stranded down here? Is prayer a *very* long-distance phone call?

From a distance

Bette Midler (and Cliff Richard, in his version) has produced what is *musically* one of my favourite songs: "From a distance". I often find myself humming the lilting melody, much to the consternation of my family, who are more than convinced that God has called me to sing as much as he has called me to be a male model: not at all.

But I've come to the conclusion that, singable though the song is, it actually reflects a subtle heresy that has caused the church and the world all kinds of grief: that "God is watching us – *from a distance*". The idea is prevalent. God is the "old man in the sky", or "the man upstairs". Wherever he is, the idea goes, he isn't here. We may be willing to concede that he was here in the past – in creation and incarnation. We may go so far as nodding to the idea that he might well just stop by in the future – in his second coming. But we can still conclude – totally wrongly – that he has effectively checked out in the meantime.

There are devastating results from that kind of "God out there" thinking. Firstly, wicked human behaviour runs riot. After all, there is no power, no moral guardian in close proximity, is there? God is at best consigned to the realm of the hereafter, managing the business of heaven, and that will take care of itself – after we die. Surely, the average Briton asserts, if there is a God, then any kind of judgment after death will be little more than a raised eyebrow, and then a free pass to heaven will be handed over; it'll all be all right on the night or the day – of judgment. But in life, he's not to be considered or reckoned with now, because, on a planet-wide basis, the Sheriff's out of town.

But the "from a distance" approach to God's proximity affects our praying too. The idea that God is "our Father in heaven" can suggest that he is located somewhere out in the wide blue yonder, perhaps slightly to the left of a distant solar system. Prayer thus becomes an exhausting attempt to fire missiles into the dark, to lob snowballs at the moon. At best we will feel like those scientists who constantly beam radio signals into deep space in the hope of a response from some passing extraterrestrials some day. It's hardly a recipe for a warm relationship. Worse, it deteriorates into an emotionally sapping experience if every time we come to worship and prayer, we are simply reaching for the stars.

> Some... think that God is a Wizard-of-Oz or
> Sistine-Chapel kind of being sitting at a location
> very remote from us. The universe is then presented
> to us chiefly as a vast empty space with a humanoid
> God and a few angels rattling around in it...
> Of such a "god" we can only say good riddance.
> It seems that when many people pray they do
> have such an image of God in their minds. They
> therefore find praying psychologically impossible or
> extremely difficult. No wonder.[21]

Hell's marketing campaign

There is dark design behind a marketing campaign designed to discredit God. Satan had consistently committed himself to the work of slandering God. The strategy goes back to Eden, when the question fashioned to undermine God's character was hissed: "Has God really said?" (Genesis 3:1).

---

21 Dallas Willard, *The Divine Conspiracy*, London: HarperCollins, 1998, p. 71.

The slander includes pumping out the message that God is absent. Indeed, the campaign has worked well, by introducing the ultimate barrier to keep a holy God distanced from his beloved created humanity – sin. *Sin* was and is the wall of estrangement (the "dividing wall of hostility") which Christ came to demolish (Ephesians 2:14), not just to alter our ultimate destination but to reconnect us with our God *now*. Sin serves Satan well: hell wants us to believe, if we have to believe at all, in a God fractured from his creation, a God departed. The madness of temptation comes to us not only to smear us with shame and defeat, but also to corral us away from God and into the despair that comes with that estrangement.

In short, it's a very bad deal indeed.

There is a second banner message in the wicked campaign to discredit God: the idea that he is impotent – or that, if he does have any power at all, he's not inclined to use it and lift a divine finger to help *us*. That's why we sometimes feel such a sense of surprise when prayer is actually answered. And, like Old Testament Israel, we are quick to forget his acts of deliverance and kindness. Indeed, we tend to forget what we should remember and remember what we should forget. God is thus portrayed as distant and uninterested. Couple this campaign with the general idea that God is geographically distant, and the result? We, humanity, feel lost in space. Permit me to quote Willard again:

> The damage done to our practical faith in Christ
> and in his government-at-hand by confusing

heaven with a place in distant or outer space or even beyond space is incalculable. Of course God is there too. But instead of heaven and God always being present with us, as Jesus shows them to be, we invariably take them to be located far away, and most likely, at a much later time – not here and not now. And should we then be surprised to feel ourselves alone?[22]

Grieving for God

When my dad died – he became a Christian in his last few years of life – I learned a very simple lesson about the nature and cause of the grief that I felt. The hollowness and overwhelming sense of loss that I experienced was not provoked by the idea of death itself. I knew that, in Christ, he was now alive. The problem was that he was now alive *elsewhere*, *departed*. When Christians lose loved ones, they are often unhelpfully told by Christian friends that they should not grieve, because the person is with Jesus now. But that was precisely my problem. He *was* and *is* with Jesus and therefore somewhere else. That means he was not – and is not – with me. There are times when I want my dad back here, now, with me, drinking a cup of tea from his favourite mug, and waxing eloquent as he did on everything that moved. Grief says: "Come back. I don't want you to be somewhere else in the universe, even if it is paradise there."

---

22 Dallas Willard, *ibid.*

No wonder the spiritualists pack in the crowd, offering as they do a link to the other side – even if God clearly warns us (Leviticus 19:31) not to set foot on that weak, dangerous, and deceptive bridge.

Indeed my dad is elsewhere. But I think that we can limit God to being in that area of the heavens too, and thus we experience a similar grief for God, believing him to be exclusively in that elsewhere domain. Thus we believe that God is alive, to be sure, and even active in some remote, distanced way – but not alive here, now, with me.

The disciples began to taste that grief with the growing realization that Jesus was going away – but he immediately encouraged them with the news that another comforter, the Holy Spirit, was coming (John 14:26). They would never be abandoned or forsaken, never again be alone (Matthew 28:20) in the universe. He is here.

Compounding the problem: come, Holy Spirit

This idea of the absent God can be fuelled by a misunderstanding of the charismatic practice of asking the Holy Spirit "to come", as if the Spirit is not present before being invited. Even if the practice of making that invitation is right (which I question), we must clearly understand that we are not asking God to be where he was previously not, and therefore to come down. To do so would imply that we need another Day of Pentecost every time we come together. Surely, when we ask the Holy Spirit to come, we are asking him to *manifest himself,* to *make his presence felt.* He acts and works generally where he is welcomed, and in praying for his coming we are, at the most, rolling out the red carpet for him and inviting his activity among us. But we are not asking God to fill a vacant space that was hitherto empty. Such an idea leaves us to walk out of those meetings to a returned state of felt emptiness and abandonment, and it obviously overstates the value of those gatherings. God becomes a localized deity who lives in the church car park: and that he certainly is not.

The reality: God, everywhere, all powerful – and *here*

So what does Jesus mean when he teaches us to pray "Our Father – in heaven"? In his gospel, Matthew uses the term "Father in heaven" twenty times.

One commentator suggests that our problem – the suggestion of a God who lives above – has been created by a poor translation of the word "heaven", which he insists should be the plural *heavens.* Suddenly, everything changes. Far from suggesting that the Father is distant, Jesus teaches precisely the opposite. The "first" heaven, biblically, is the atmosphere or air that immediately surrounds your body. Jesus is teaching us here that God the Father is in all and is all in all – right near us, and right out there both. He is introducing us to the infinite, omnipresent Father who is so very, very close, and in whom we "live and move and have our being" (Acts 17:28).

Matthew is also giving us widescreen vision of the Lord, banishing our dwarfed godlets with the revelation that we have a Father whose authority and presence stretches across the heavens and the earth. And this truth is far more than abstract theology, but reaches down into our Monday morning praying. It means that we have authority to participate in the unfolding drama of history-making, as we partner with God through our prayers.

Love does make the world go round

God is near. That affects our understanding of the world around us. We have evolved an idea that there are "laws" of nature – which seems to imply that there is a cold-hearted mechanic, or nerdy scientist, at the heart of the universe. Nature becomes not an ongoing act of creation and sustenance, but a machine of necessity. James Bryan Smith writes of his discovery that there is a passionate artist at the centre of it all. It is not that he was interested, but isn't any longer. He is actively splashing his paint and moulding his clay all over the place.

> G.K. Chesterton changed the way I look at the
> world around me. He pointed out that nature
> is not a system of necessity. Yes, the sun will
> probably come up tomorrow, but it need not.
> Perhaps each day God says to the sun, "Arise! Go

forth!" Yes, grass is typically green, but it need not be. God could make it purple if he wished. There are no "laws" of nature. Frogs jump and birds fly and water runs down hill not because of laws but because, writes Chesterton, God wishes them to do so.[23]

Divine graffiti

It's been said that most of what God does, he does behind our backs. We all like to give the impression that we know what God is doing. Most of the time, we haven't a clue. Once in a while, we catch a hint of his work, shout loudly about our brilliant discovery, and, in the case of those of us who write, probably dash off another book about it. God is near, but he doesn't always consult. In other words, he is at work in a billion ways this very second that we cannot even fathom. It is a grave mistake, for example, to see mission as something that starts in the initiative and heart of the church – that leads us to exhausting, sweaty effort. Rather, our task is to connect with that which God is already doing in *his* mission, the *missio Dei* – the mission of God. And sometimes God's fingerprints are to be found in the most unusual places: he is constantly at play across the earth.

He is very much here, and not only when he is acknowledged or noticed. That helps me to understand why a piece of gloriously inventive music may be written

23 James Bryan Smith, *A Little Handbook of God's Love*, London: Hodder and Stoughton, 2000, p. 15.

by someone who doesn't know God. I can admire the masterful use of colour and shade on canvas, the work of an artist whose heart is in the far country and yet who has been kissed, though they don't know it, by the touch of the Creator. Shall I ascribe the source of their creativity to Satan? I will not, because we are living in a God-bathed world. I caught a glimpse of his inspiration when I watched the film *The Truman Show.* Jim Carrey – Truman – bumps into the edge of his artificial world. He didn't know it, but he had spent his whole life in a reality that was false, because it was a huge television studio. As in *The Matrix*, Truman discovers that there is a bigger reality beyond the artificial confines of the studio. Will he walk through the door to the real life? Or will he listen to the dark voice that taunts him: "There's nothing more out there, Truman"? Will he continue to play the myth-game? The whole world cheers as Truman walks through the door into true life. Was God listed on the movie credits? On the contrary. But I believe that he was making his presence felt in the crafting of that film, the invisible director and scriptwriter, prophetically prompting the questions of life through art, scribbling his signature in unexpected places.

God – very much here, and our provider

The immediacy of God also says something to us about our approach to the provision of our daily needs. Jesus paints a portrait of a close-up God who is actively involved in every

detail of life on the planet. He is revealed as the One who
knows us intimately, knowing what we need before we even
ask him (Matthew 6:8). The fact that God not only can
be known, but that *he knows us*, is foundational to biblical
revelation. To each of the seven churches of Revelation,
walking as they did through a dark season of pressure, with
the clouds of persecution gathering on the near horizon,
Jesus says, "I know" (Revelation 2:2, 9, 13, 19; 3:1, 8, 15).
We are therefore not impersonal digits or numbers in a
database, lost in the crowd, but each of us is known by
God. His knowledge of us and his closeness to us lead us
to expect and anticipate his hand at work in daily provision
for our lives.

> Therefore I tell you, do not worry about your life,
> what you will eat or drink; or about your body,
> what you will wear. Is not life more important than
> food, and the body more important than clothes?
> Look at the birds of the air; they do not sow or
> reap or store away in barns, and yet your heavenly
> Father feeds them. Are you not much more
> valuable than they? Who of you by worrying can
> add a single hour to his life?
>
> And why do you worry about clothes? See
> how the lilies of the field grow. They do not labour
> or spin. Yet I tell you that not even Solomon in all
> his splendour was dressed like one of these. If that
> is how God clothes the grass of the field, which is
> here today and tomorrow is thrown into the fire,
> will he not much more clothe you, O you of little
> faith? So do not worry, saying, 'What shall we eat?'

or 'What shall we drink?' or 'What shall we wear?'
For the pagans run after all these things, and your
heavenly Father knows that you need them. But
seek first his kingdom and his righteousness, and all
these things will be given to you as well. Therefore
do not worry about tomorrow, for tomorrow will
worry about itself. Each day has enough trouble of
its own. (Matthew 6:25–34)

Concluding: the God who dwells with us

As we draw this discussion on the close-up God to an
end, we must remember that the very foundation of the
Christian faith is an invitation to live in, abide in, and
rest in the here-and-now presence of God. Without him
we really can do nothing (John 15:5) – and his closeness
and dynamic activism in our lives is the only way that we
can experience real transformation. We may tinker and
mess around with the external behaviour and bits of our
lives, but only he can get inside us and do a work of true
change. He is at our side. C. S. Lewis reminds us that,
fundamentally, we are but "tin soldiers".

> Our faith is not a matter of our hearing what
> Christ said long ago and trying to carry it out. The
> real Son of God is at your side. He is beginning to
> turn you into the same kind of thing as Himself.
> He is beginning, so to speak, to 'inject' His kind of
> life and thought, His *Zoe* [life] into you; beginning

to turn the tin soldier into a live man. The part of
you that does not like it is the part that is still tin.[24]

God is not the One who is watching us from a distance
and for whom our shouts and sobs can be scarcely heard
or understood. On the contrary, you, right where you are,
right now, are hemmed in and surrounded by your loving
heavenly Father. And so St Patrick prayed:

> *Christ to protect me today*
> *against poison, against burning,*
> *against drowning, against wounding,*
> *so that there may come abundance of reward.*
>
> *Christ with me, Christ before me,*
> *Christ in me, Christ beneath me, Christ above me,*
> *Christ on my right, Christ on my left,*
> *Christ where I lie, Christ where I sit, Christ where*
>   *I arise,*
> *Christ in the heart of every man who thinks of me,*
> *Christ in the mouth of every man who speaks of me,*
> *Christ in every eye that sees me,*
> *Christ in every ear that hears me.[25]*

---

24 *Mere Christianity* by C. S. Lewis copyright © C. S. Lewis Pte. Ltd. 1942,
1943, 1944, 1952. Extract reprinted by permission.
25 Ludwig Bieler, *The Works of St. Patrick*, Mahwah: Paulist Press, 1978.

7

Prayer: it's not just about us

"Hallowed be your name, your kingdom come, your will be done on earth as it is in heaven."

"We have de-clawed the Lion of Judah and made him a house cat for pale priests."

– Dorothy L. Sayers

Beware low-flying cornflakes...

Kay has banned me from viewing certain Christian television programmes. It would be churlish to mention which, but this viewing prohibition has been so ordered because she is weary of the sight of breakfast cereal dripping down the front of the television set. Why is it that some of my hottest moments of boiling rage centre around these anonymous programmes? Yes, I feel pastorally aggrieved (what a noble-sounding description for my anger) when I hear preachers take a superficial approach to suffering and slap those who suffer with slogans. But my frustration is mainly provoked by the message that is pumped out with cereal-wasting regularity: the gospel is all about *me* getting *my* dreams fulfilled, and I need to "use" Jesus for that purpose. Whatever I want in life, he's the key. Dream away, says the preacher. Dream on, say I.

Teaching of this type not only does violence to Scripture, but also creates a warped portrait of God. Jesus is reduced to being like Santa, with a cross instead of a sleigh. The challenging news that I might be called to lose my life (Matthew 10:39) or to make his kingdom my first priority seems lost. This approach to Christianity, with its easy formulae, trivializes the sublime, ignores the need to trust God in the place of mystery, and portrays God as a cosmic vending machine, urgently plied with intercessory tokens when you spot that new car you'd like. Like a virus, it spreads the idea that if you're not rich or brimming with health, then you're spiritually blighted. It is an unjust, unwarranted slap in the face for the vast majority of the world who won't eat today. Now, not only are their stomachs empty, but their faith is second-rate too. The absurd idea is that they are cursed with a poverty of faith. Forgive my bluntness, but it needs to be said: this is vomit-inducing stuff. But it's not only extreme health-and-wealth teaching that gives the impression that God primarily exists to give me the stuff that I crave. There are more subtle approaches to prayer that give the impression that the pathway of prayer is a predictable road, and if you follow certain principles or laws, then you will always get the same "result".

Prayer: not a mechanistic formula for *me*

I admit to being nervous of the "Seven laws for blessing in your life" approach, simply because it is so impersonal, and I don't believe that any relationship – including one with God – can be reduced to laws and abstract principles. There is no real intimacy, no foundation of love and laughter, just a process towards a result, a means to an end. It centres on the gift rather than the giver, and treats God like a heavenly supermarket check-out operator.

As we hear Jesus begin to talk about God's name being hallowed, and his kingdom and his will breaking out in the earth, we discover that when it comes to requests, we find ourselves second in line. Put simply, prayer is not just about me: on the contrary.

No neutral spirituality

We are scarcely a sentence into the model prayer of Jesus, and we immediately bump into the rule, reign, and authority of God. We have barely tiptoed into his presence, and before we've had the chance to say much at all we have to acknowledge the reality of a moral, spiritual power that is beyond ourselves. There is a popular spirituality that is available today – perhaps it's always been available – that comforts us, helps us to realize our dreams or to discover our cosmic significance, but that makes absolutely no demands upon us. It only brings solace; no sacrifice is involved. It involves us finding the god of our choosing, one that we ultimately can make in our own image. This god is superficially lovely rather than intrinsically loving, and will never challenge our selfishness, hedonism or greed. But Jesus refuses to allow us to make him into our good-luck charm, a divine rabbit's foot or any other kind of talisman. As we come to him, we confess that he is King and Lord.

There is nothing abstract or vague about that confession. We come willing to see his rule and order as the very first priority in our lives. But let's remember, if that sounds a little too austere, as if there were a control freak at the heart of the universe, that God brings order *because* he loves. What kind of loving father would sit silent in the face of chaos breaking out in the lives of his children, without wanting to restore the order and peace that his rule can bring? We quickly collide with the truth of his kingdom reign, yet this is not the rod of iron gripped in the fist of a dictator, but the storm-calming rule of peace ushered in by the greatest Father there has ever been.

God's kingdom rule is good – the best. To live under it is to experience liberation and joy – if that is not the case, then how can we really pray sincerely that others will come under it? What prisoner would hope that others would get to experience the damp near-starvation of the cell, and torture at the hands of his guards? He would be mad to pray that others would taste the oppression that is crushing him. No, the good rule of the good God is breathtakingly wonderful. As we taste that, we can hope and pray that others will find it too.

The priority of his name: let it be hallowed

Talk of names being "hallowed" is foreign to our ears. Our most likely familiarity with something being *hallowed* is probably *Hallowe'en,* the All Saints' evening of old. But surely God's name *is* holy, and won't become more holy because of our prayers. Yet in asking that God's name be hallowed, we are asking that his name might be seen as worthy of respect and honour – a vital prayer in a culture that has demoted the name of Jesus Christ to the level of a swear word. I heard recently of a child who attended a church service and was shocked to hear the minister "swearing". The confused parents discovered that their son was bewildered because the priest had said the words *Jesus Christ* during the liturgy – words that, as far as he knew, were only used in swearing.

In ancient times great importance was invested into a name – indeed the name of God was so revered that we really don't know how to properly pronounce *Yahweh* today. A person's name was synonymous with their reputation and character: to defame someone's name was a very serious act.

It goes without saying – yet we must own the tragedy of it – that the name of Jesus Christ has been consistently misrepresented, maligned, and smeared. And though it gives me no pleasure to confess it, this smearing has often been because of the foolishness of the Christians – who bear his name. As a result of our poor advocacy, he has been pronounced guilty without a trial, dismissed as irrelevant because, so often, we the church have disguised him as tedious, mainly because we have been so unappealing. This was no small feat for us and our churchly ancestors – taking the most brilliant, luminous personality in the history of the universe, dulling and dumbing him down. But, alas, we have done it, and done it all too effectively.

Dorothy L. Sayers laments the damage done to the name and the person of Christ:

> The people who crucified Jesus did not do so
> because he was a bore; quite the contrary. He was
> too dynamic to be safe. It has been left for later
> generations to muffle up that shattering personality,
> and surround him with an atmosphere of tedium.
> We have de-clawed the Lion of Judah and made
> him a house cat for pale priests.

But all is not lost: we are those who are still privileged to say, "Your name be hallowed." Perhaps this is the prayer of *alarm* that a child might feel if someone suggested that their parents were dishonourable.

When I was in secondary school, there was a particularly obnoxious chap who was acid-tongued with his insults and derision. In any war of words (and there were many skirmishes in our playground) his favourite tactical insult was to say "Your mother is a prostitute." He used the insult so frequently, an observer might have concluded that half of our school were the offspring of ladies of the night. As we might expect, that particular sneering accusation always signalled a black eye for him. He could say whatever he liked about us – but tarnish the honour of our mothers? Break out the bandages. You would have thought that he would have learned. He never did. He spent most of his schooldays looking like a badger.

I'm not sure about those undeniably sincere people who go around tersely correcting everyone who blasphemes or misuses the name of Jesus. The end result of the rebuke might not necessarily lead to any positive fruit. Yet there are times (perhaps) to protest when the name of the One that we love is maligned and misused. But surely our prayer that the name of God should be honoured goes deeper than concern about swearing. We are praying that those who feel lost in life will discover the direction and love that is only available "in the name". When God's name is defiled, the signpost that can lead the wandering home is defaced and vandalized. And that matters.

This name is the source of salvation, and so we pray that the real truth will come out about it and the One who owns it. Notice that our prayer is immediately focused outward, towards a dark world. Why? Because God weeps for the emptiness of the wandering, and longs that the signpost of his name might be cleaned up. In a post-modern age of pluralism and relativism, we affirm the biblical insistence that life is only available in one name. By it alone can those stranded in sin's blizzard come in from the cold.

Andrei Bitov is a Russian writer who describes the day he found that warm welcome:

In my twenty-seventh year, while riding the Metro in Leningrad, I was overcome with a despair so great that life seemed to stop at once, pre-empting the future entirely, let alone any meaning. Suddenly, all by itself, a phrase appeared: without God life makes no sense. Repeating it in astonishment, I rode the phrase up like a moving staircase, got out of the Metro and walked into God's light.[26]

Prayer in the real world

Praying that is closeted away from the pressing needs of the world isn't worth a lot; mission is at the heart of the praying that God smiles upon. Before we have said anything else much, we have been invited to look outward to a world that defames the Great Name. We have looked upward, to "our Father in the heavens", and then immediately we look outward at the lost world that is so loved of the Father.

We learn here that our church gatherings should be linked into the pulse of what is happening beyond her cloistered walls. Church was never designed to be an escape act, a trip to spiritual Disneyland that enables us to forget the hurting, wounded, and wounding world in which we all live.

Lynn Green painfully shared recently about a charismatic meeting that he attended just a few miles from Bethlehem

---

26 Quoted in David Friend (ed.), *The Meaning of Life*, Boston: Little, Brown, 1991, p. 194.

while an infamous siege raged on, in which people were killed. Palestinians – including a number of Christians – were being shelled by Israeli tanks. Just a few thousand yards away, Christians got together for another Holy Spirit top-up without any reference to the blood and tears that were being shed so close to where they met. Spirituality that turns its back on the world isn't worth any time or effort.

The priority of his kingdom and his will: let it come

Having prayed about the name of God, we are blessed with the authority to say, "Your kingdom come, your will be done." These words are often misunderstood to refer exclusively to the second coming of Christ and our future in the eternal kingdom of God – the proverbial "pie in the sky when you die" thinking. The confusion is compounded further by Matthew's use of the term "kingdom of heaven", which again causes us to hastily conclude that he is talking about something that will be *later*. But Matthew used the phrase "kingdom of heaven" because he was writing to Jews and so used the common Jewish terminology of the day. The other Gospels avoid this term because it would have been meaningless to the Gentiles.

In short, I want us to see that praying that the kingdom will come is about what's going on today, tomorrow, and next Monday morning – *and* it's also about the ultimate future. One day the fullness, consummation, and totality of God's kingdom reign will be found in the return of Christ, but in the meantime we are able to call for the kingdom of God to break out today through a thousand different apertures. A smile in the office, a moment of kindness at the school gate, a comment that brings light into darkness in the college corridor, the calling for a zebra crossing in that accident black spot – in these moments, as we call for righteousness, the right order of God, to prevail, so the kingdom relentlessly ripples outward.

Let's take a moment to explore the kingdom a little more. It's a neglected theme, but it's so core to our praying and our understanding of where we fit in God's purposes.

Recovering the kingdom

The "kingdom" was the main teaching theme of the ministry of Jesus. The heartbeat of the Sermon on the Mount is found in the command, "Seek first the kingdom of God" (Matthew 6:33). Jesus' travelling, preaching, and teaching ministry had the kingdom as its core theme – he went about "preaching the good news of the kingdom" (Matthew 4:23). Michael Green remarks: "The kingdom was Jesus' prime concern."[27] Matthew uses the term thirty-two times. So how come we haven't heard more about the kingdom from our pulpits? Dr I. Howard Marshall echoes this concern about kingdom silence when he points out that in the past sixteen

---

27 Quoted in Tom Sine, *The Mustard Seed Conspiracy*, Nashville: W Pub. Group, 1981, pp. 102–103.

years he has only heard two sermons specifically devoted to the theme of the kingdom of God, despite the fact that New Testament scholars all agree the kingdom of God was the central theme of Jesus' teaching. It is a tragedy that we have subdued the kingdom shout of Jesus to the faintest whisper.

The kingdom: the arena of his reign and rule

The biblical words for kingdom are *malkuth* (Hebrew) and *basileia* (Greek). The meaning of these words is primarily "rule" or "reign" rather than "realm". In other words, when we speak of God's kingdom, we are thinking about the arena of his rule and command, rather than any kind of geographical location. Perhaps that's why our minds struggle: we are familiar with the idea of a king or queen reigning over an area of land – their geographical *kingdom* – rather than thinking of a kingdom in terms of the area of their rule and influence.

The term "kingdom of God" does not appear in the Old Testament directly, but the long-awaited kingship of God was the hope and theme song of the prophets. God was seen as king over Israel and also over the whole earth – but the Old Testament also speaks of a day when he shall *become* king (Isaiah 24:23, 52:7; Zephaniah 3:15; Zechariah 14:9ff). That's a helpful illustration of the "It's here, but there's more" truth of the kingdom. God is already king, but he will yet be king in greater fullness – in the fullness of time.

And then... the odd chap in the wilderness shows up

John the Baptist, alarmingly noticeable with his odd fashion choices and his worrying habit of snacking on grasshoppers, suddenly came on the scene and lobbed a verbal wake-up call at his listeners. "Repent, for the kingdom of heaven is at hand" (Matthew 3:2). He came in the line of the Old Testament prophets, standing on tiptoe, proclaiming that the kingdom was about to come among them – and so a radical response of repentance was required from those who listened to this oddest of preachers. John conducted much of his ministry in the desert, traditionally the place of restoration for Israel. The message was bubbling with anticipation – something or somebody very, very big was about to step onto the stage of human history. And then he came.

Jesus and the kingdom

Jesus arrived preaching the same message as his cousin John, but with the added phrase, a dramatic addendum to John's wake-up call, "The time is fulfilled" (Mark 1:15). John had spoken at the eleventh hour – but with Jesus, the clock struck midnight. In the synagogue, he says, "*Today* this Scripture is fulfilled" (Luke 4:21). Already the messianic banquet had begun. It was a time for feasting, not fasting: the bridegroom was here, and the new wine was flowing.